my revision notes

Edexcel GCSE

MATHEMATICS REVISION GUIDE

FOUNDATION

Gareth Cole
Karen Hughes
Joe Petran
Keith Pledger

HODDER
EDUCATION
AN HACHETTE UK COMPANY

The Publishers would like to thank the following for permission to reproduce copyright material.

Acknowledgements

Every effort has been made to trace all copyright holders, but if any have been inadvertently overlooked, the Publishers will be pleased to make the necessary arrangements at the first opportunity.

Although every effort has been made to ensure that website addresses are correct at time of going to press, Hodder Education cannot be held responsible for the content of any website mentioned in this book. It is sometimes possible to find a relocated web page by typing in the address of the home page for a website in the URL window of your browser.

Hachette UK's policy is to use papers that are natural, renewable and recyclable products and made from wood grown in sustainable forests. The logging and manufacturing processes are expected to conform to the environmental regulations of the country of origin.

Orders

Bookpoint Ltd, 130 Park Drive, Milton Park, Abingdon, Oxon OX14 4SE.
Telephone: (44) 01235 827720.
Fax: (44) 01235 400454.
Email education@bookpoint.co.uk
Lines are open from 9 a.m. to 5 p.m., Monday to Saturday, with a 24-hour message answering service. You can also order through our website: www.hoddereducation.co.uk

ISBN: 978 1 4718 8246 3

First published in 2016 by

Hodder Education,
An Hachette UK Company
Carmelite House
50 Victoria Embankment
London EC4Y 0DZ
www.hoddereducation.co.uk

Impression number   10 9 8 7 6 5 4 3 2 1

Year   2019 2018 2017 2016

Cover photo © Les Wagstaff/Alamy Stock Photo
Typeset in Integra Software Services Pvt Ltd, Pondicherry, India
Printed in Spain

A catalogue record for this title is available from the British Library.

Get the most from this book

Welcome to your Revision Guide for the Edexcel GCSE Mathematics (9-1) Foundation course. This book will provide you with sound summaries of the knowledge and skills you will be expected to demonstrate in the exam, with additional hints and techniques on every page. Throughout the book, you will also find a wealth of additional support to ensure that you feel confident and fully prepared for your GCSE Maths Foundation examination.

This Revision Guide is divided into four main sections, with additional support at the back of the book. The four main sections cover the four mathematical themes that will be covered in your course and examined: Number, Algebra, Geometry & Measure and Statistics & Probability.

Features to help you succeed

Each theme is broken down into one-page topics as shown in this example:

The knowledge you have learned on your course is reduced to the key rules for this topic area. You will need to understand and remember these for your exam.

Worked examples are provided to remind you how the rules work. Each rule is highlighted next to where it is being used.

Exam-style questions provide real practice on the topic area, with allocated marks so you can see the level of response that is required.

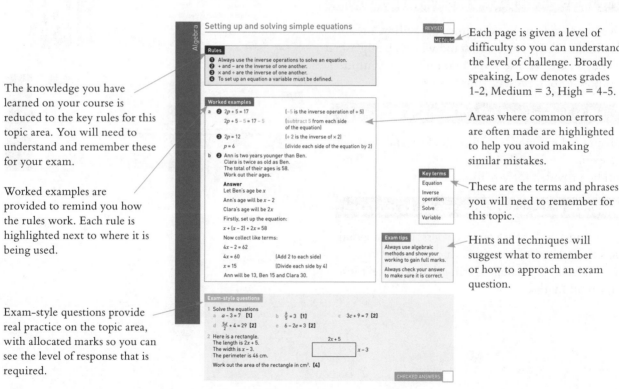

Each page is given a level of difficulty so you can understand the level of challenge. Broadly speaking, Low denotes grades 1-2, Medium = 3, High = 4-5.

Areas where common errors are often made are highlighted to help you avoid making similar mistakes.

These are the terms and phrases you will need to remember for this topic.

Hints and techniques will suggest what to remember or how to approach an exam question.

Each theme section also includes the following:

Pre-revision check

Each section begins with a test of questions covering each topic within that theme. This is a helpful place to start to see if there are any areas which you may need to pay particular attention to in your revision. To make it easier, we have included the page reference for each topic page next to the question, and also the page reference to the relevant Mastering Mathematics Student Book.

Exam-style question tests

There are two sets of tests made up of practice exam-style questions to help you check your progress as you go along. These can be found midway through and at the end of each theme. You will find **Answers** to these tests at the back of the book.

At the end of the book, you will find some very useful information provided by our assessment experts:

The language used in mathematics examinations

This page explains the wording that will be used in the exam to help you understand what is being asked of you. There are also some extra hints to remind you how to best present your answers.

Exam technique and formulae that will be given

A list of helpful advice for both before and during the exams, and confirmation of the formulae that will be provided for you in the exams.

Common areas where students make mistakes

These pages will help you to understand and avoid the common misconceptions that students sitting past exams have made, ensuring that you don't lose important marks.

One week to go....

Reminders and formulae for you to remember in the final days before the exam.

Tick to track your progress

Use the revision planner on pages v to viii to plan your revision, topic by topic. Tick each box when you have:
● worked through the pre-revision check
● revised the topic
● checked your answers

You can also keep track of your revision by ticking off each topic heading in the book. You may find it helpful to add your own notes as you work through each topic.

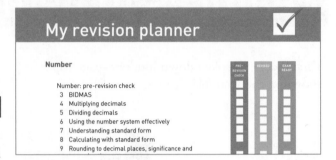

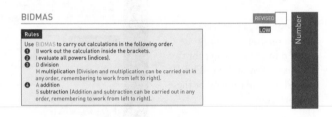

My revision planner

Number

Algebra

REVISED

EXAM READY

Geometry and Measures

Statistics and Probability

Exam preparation

PRE-REVISION CHECK

REVISED

EXAM READY

Number: pre-revision check

Check how well you know each topic by answering these questions. If you get a question wrong, go to the page number in brackets to revise that topic.

1 Work out
  a $5 + 7 \div 2$
  b 2×3^2
  c $\frac{16 - 4.1}{2.6 + 5.9}$ (page 3)

2 Work out
  a 3.174×8
  b 12.6×4.5 (page 4)

3 Work out
  a $10.44 \div 0.4$
  b $42.208 \div 1.6$ (page 5)

4 Work out
  a 1.8×0.01
  b $12.45 \div 0.1$
  c 254.9×1000
  d $0.00487 \div 0.0001$ (page 6)

5 a Write 0.00572 in standard form.
  b Write 3.184×10^4 as an ordinary number.
  (page 7)

6 Work out
  a $(1.5 \times 10^3) \div (2.8 \times 10^{-1})$
  b $(9.42 \times 10^2) + (1.36 \times 10^3)$ (page 8)

7 Write 16.3548 correct to
  a 1 decimal place
  b 2 decimal places
  c 3 decimal places.   (page 9)

8 Write 0.001 5472 correct to
  a 1 significant figure
  b 2 significant figures
  c 3 significant figures.   (page 9)

9 Write down an estimate for the value of
  a 3201
  b 0.0029   (page 9)

10 A number is given as 8.37 correct to 2 decimal places. Write down the lower and upper bounds of this number.   (page 10)

11 Work out
  a $\frac{4}{9} \times \frac{5}{8}$
  b $\frac{1}{3} \times \frac{4}{11} \times \frac{9}{20}$
  c $6 \div \frac{2}{3}$
  d $\frac{15}{42} \div \frac{5}{7}$ (page 11)

12 Work out
  a $\frac{7}{12} - \frac{2}{5}$
  b $3 + \frac{3}{4} - \frac{1}{3}$
  c $10\frac{2}{3} + 7\frac{3}{5}$
  d $3\frac{4}{7} \times 2\frac{4}{5}$ (page 12)
  e $2\frac{1}{10} \div 1\frac{3}{4}$ (page 11)

13 a Convert to a percentage
  i $\frac{11}{20}$
  ii 1.9.
  b Convert 6% to a
  i fraction
  ii decimal.   (page 13)

14 a Increase £12.50 by 4%.
  b Decrease 550 m by 32%.   (page 14)

15 a Work out 20 cm as a percentage of 2.5 m.
  b A clock is bought for £72 and sold for £54. What is the percentage loss?   (page 15)

16 The average cost of a new house in Brinton has increased by 6%. The average cost is now £118 720. What was the average cost before this increase?   (page 16)

17 £20 000 is invested in a bank paying compound interest at a rate of 3.4% each year. Work out the value of this investment after 4 years.   (page 17)

18 a Divide 280 m in the ratio 3:5.
  b Alfie, Bernice and Charlie share a sum of money in the ratio 1:3:5. What fraction of the money does Charlie get? (page 19)

19 Five identical spheres weigh a total of 1.235 kg. Find the total weight of eight of these spheres. (page 20)

20 Which of these tables of values illustrates direct proportion and which illustrate inverse proportion? (page 21)

x	1	2	5	12	20
y	300	150	60	25	15

x	10	20	30	40	50
y	2.5	5	7.5	10	12.5

x	0.1	0.2	0.3	0.4	0.5
y	180	90	60	45	36

21 T is inversely proportional to x. When $x = 1.4$, $P = 25$. Write down a formula for T in terms of x. (page 22)

22 Write each of these as a power of 3
  a $(3^4 \times 3^3) \div 3^2$
  b $3^8 \div (3^2 \times 3)$
  c $(3^5 \times 3^4)^2$ (page 23)

23 Work out the value of the following:
  a $(2^4 \div 2^{-3}) \times 2^{-5}$
  b $(10^9 \times 10^{-4} \div 10^3)^2$ (page 23)

24 Write 1260 as a product of its prime factors. (page 24)

BIDMAS

Rules

Use **BIDMAS** to carry out calculations in the following order.
1. **B** work out the calculation inside the brackets.
2. **I** evaluate all powers (indices).
3. **D** division
   M multiplication (Division and multiplication can be carried out in any order, remembering to work from left to right).
4. **A** addition
   S subtraction (Addition and subtraction can be carried out in any order, remembering to work from left to right).

Worked examples

a Work out $2^4 \times 10 + (15 - 7) \div 4$

Answer

1. $= 2^4 \times 10 + 8 \div 4$ $(15 - 7 = 8)$
2. $= 16 \times 10 + 8 \div 4$ $(2^4 = 16)$
3. $= 160 + 2$ $(16 \times 10 = 160$ and $8 \div 4 = 2)$
4. $= 160 + 2 = 162$

b Use your calculator to work out $\dfrac{5.63 + 12.17}{19.26 - 4.9}$

Answer

$$\frac{5.63 + 12.17}{19.26 - 4.9} = \frac{17.8}{14.36}$$
$$= 1.239$$

(17.8 is the value of the numerator)
(14.36 is the value of the denominator)

Key terms

Brackets

Indices

Operation

Exam tip

Work out the value of the numerator and the denominator first.

Exam-style questions

1. **a** Work out $12 - 4 \times 2$ **[1]**
   b Put brackets where appropriate to make this statement true. $3 + 9 - 5 \times 2 = 11$ **[1]**
2. Here are 5 different symbols $\div$ $($ $+$ $-$ $)$
   Use each symbol once only to make this statement true.
   7 10 3 2 = 5 **[2]**

3. Use your calculator to work out $\dfrac{1.5^2 + 3.6}{7.4 - \sqrt{1.44}}$ **[2]**

Exam tips

Check by using the rules of BIDMAS.

Multiplying decimals

Rules

1. To start any calculation, first ignore the decimal points.
2. Carry out the multiplication of whole numbers by your preferred method.
3. Make sure the decimal point in your answer is in the correct place.

Worked examples

a One metre of wood weighs 3.56 kg.

Work out the weight of 0.6 metres of this wood.

Answer

1. Ignore the decimal points and work out 356×6

2.
```
  3 5 6
×     6
─────────
2 1 3 6
  3 3
```

3.
$$3.56 \quad \times \quad 0.6 \quad = \quad 2.136 \text{ kg}$$

2 decimal places + 1 decimal place = 3 decimal places

b Work out 15.3×1.9

Answer

1. Ignore the decimal points and work out 153×19

2.
	100	50	3	
10	1000	500	30	Adding gives 1530
9	900	450	27	Adding gives 1377 +
				2907

3. $5.3 \times 1.9 = 29.07$ (since the answer is about 30)

Key terms

Decimal point

Decimal places

Exam tip

Work out an estimate

15.3 is about 15

1.9 is about 2

$15 \times 2 = 30$;

so the answer will be about 30

Exam-style questions

1 Work out 439×1.4 **[3]**

2 Jermaine wants to buy 120 roses as cheaply as possible.
Shop A sells 10 roses for £5.36. Shop B sells 6 roses for £3.24.

From which shop should Jermaine buy the 120 roses? **[4]**

3 The electricity readings at the start and the end of a 3-month period were 502.7 kWh and 547.3 kWh.
Electricity costs 23.5 p/kWh.
Work out total cost of the electricity used in this 3-month period. **[4]**

Exam tip

Clearly label your working for shop A or shop B. Write your final answer in a sentence, showing clearly the two total costs **or** the cost of each rose from shop A and shop B.

CHECKED ANSWERS

Dividing decimals

Rules

❶ Rearrange the calculation so that you are dividing by a whole number.

❷ Carry out the division by the whole number by your preferred method.

❸ To get more decimal places in your answer, add zeros to the decimal number you are dividing.

Worked examples

a The area of a rectangle is 4.252 square metres.

Work out the length of the rectangle if the width is 0.8 metres.

Answer

$4.252 \times 10 = 42.52$

and $0.8 \times 10 = 8$

❶ so $4.252 \div 0.8$ is the same as $42.52 \div 8$

❷
$$\begin{array}{r} 5.315 \\ 8\overline{)42.5^{2}5^{1}2^{4}0} \end{array}$$

Add a 0 to the remainder of 4 and then divide 40 by 8

so length = 5.315 metres

b Work out $146.4 \div 0.16$

Answer

❶ $146.4 \div 0.16$ is the same as $14640 \div 16$

❷
$$\begin{array}{r} 91.5 \\ 16\overline{)14640} \\ -\underline{144} \\ 24 \\ -\underline{16} \\ 80 \\ -\underline{80} \\ 0 \end{array}$$

$1 \times 16 = 16$
$2 \times 16 = 32$
$3 \times 16 = 48$
$4 \times 16 = 64$
$5 \times 16 = 80$
$6 \times 16 = 96$
$7 \times 16 = 112$
$8 \times 16 = 128$
$9 \times 16 = 144$

> **Exam tip**
>
> Multiply each number in this case by 10, so that you divide by whole numbers

> **Key terms**
>
> Decimal point
>
> Decimal places

> **Exam tip**
>
> (to help with long division)
>
> Write down the first 9 multiples of the number you are dividing by (16 in this example)

Exam-style questions

1 Five identical pens cost £39.60

Work out the cost of one pen. **[2]**

2 A rope is 5.32 metres in length.

How many 0.8 metre pieces can be cut from this rope? **[2]**

3 Jane buys a car.
She agrees to pay a deposit of £1500 and 36 equal monthly instalments.
In total she will have to pay £10 629.60

Work out the cost of each monthly instalment. **[4]**

> **Exam tips**
>
> Set out your working clearly.
>
> Check that your answers are realistic.

CHECKED ANSWERS

Using the number system effectively

Rules

In order for the place value of each digit to be correct:
1. When multiplying by 0.1 or 0.01 or 0.001, etc. move the decimal point 1, 2 or 3 places, etc. to the LEFT. This is the same as dividing by 10 or 100 or 1000, etc. The answer will be **smaller** in value.
2. When dividing by 0.1 or 0.01 or 0.001, etc. move the decimal point 1, 2 or 3 places, etc. to the RIGHT. This is the same as multiplying by 10 or 100 or 1000, etc. The answer will be **greater** in value.

Worked examples

a Work out
   i 34.29×0.1
   ii $34.29 \div 0.1$
   iii 34.29×1000
   iv $34.29 \div 0.0001$

Answers
1. i $34.29 \times 0.1 = 3.429$ ← one place to the left
2. ii $34.29 \div 0.1 = 342.9$ → one place to the right
2. iii $34.29 \times 1000 = 34290$ ← three places to the right
      (one 0 was added to 34.29)
2. iv $34.29 \div 0.0001 = 342900$ → four places to the right
      (two 0s were added to 34.29)

b Given that $52.4 \times 3.75 = 196.5$, work out
   i 5.24×0.375
   ii $19.65 \div 0.524$

Answers
1. $5.24 = 52.4 \div 10$ (or $\times 0.1$)
   $0.375 = 3.75 \div 10$ (or $\times 0.1$)
   So $5.24 \times 0.375 = 196.5 \div 10 \div 10$
               $= 1.965$
1. $19.65 = 196.5 \div 10$ (or $\times 0.1$)
   $0.524 = 52.4 \div 100$ (or $\times 0.01$)
   So $19.65 \div 0.524 = \frac{196.5 \div 10}{52.5 \div 100}$

      $= 3.75 \times 10 = 37.5$

Key term

Place value

Exam tip

Your answer will contain the same digits as the value in the question, e.g. 1965 in bi and 375 in bii.

Exam-style questions

1 Here is an input/output machine.

input ⟶ ×0.01 ⟶ ÷10 ⟶ output

   a Work out the output when the input is 539 **[2]**
   b Work out the input when the output is 4.58 **[2]**

2 Given that $119 \times 0.35 = 41.65$ work out:
   a 11.9×350 **[1]**
   b $0.4165 \div 0.035$ **[1]**
   c 11.9×0.07 **[2]**

Exam tip

Use inverse operations when given the output.

Look out for

Use the rules above to check that you have not placed decimal points in the wrong place.

CHECKED ANSWERS

Understanding standard form

MEDIUM

Rules

To write a number in standard form:
1. Move the decimal point a number of places so that it is immediately after the first non-zero digit and multiply by a suitable power of 10.
2. If the decimal point has been moved to the left, the power of 10 will be plus the number of places moved.
3. If the decimal point has been moved to the right, the power of 10 will be minus the number of places moved.

Key terms

Standard form

Ordinary number

Powers

Worked examples

a Write these numbers in standard form.
   i 347 000
   ii 0.002 18

Answers
i $347\,000 = 347\,000.0 = 3.47 \times 10^?$

   5 places to the left

   2 means a power of +5

   $347\,000 = 3.47 \times 10^5$

ii $0.002\,18 = 2.18 \times 10^?$

   3 places to the right

   3 means a power of −3

   $0.002\,18 = 2.18 \times 10^{-3}$

Exam tips

If the number is large, the power will be positive.

If the number is small, the power will be negative.

b Which number has the greater value, 1.75×10^{-9} or 8.19×10^{-10}?

Answer
$1.75 \times 10^{-9} = 0.000\,000\,001\,75$ (moving the decimal point 9 places to the left (reverse of 3; note 9 zeros))

$8.19 \times 10^{-10} = 0.000\,000\,000\,819$ (moving the decimal point 10 places to the left (reverse of 3; note 10 zeros))

$0.000\,000\,001\,75$ is greater than $0.000\,000\,000\,819$

Exam tip

Change numbers into ordinary numbers by following the rules above in reverse.

Exam-style questions

1 Write these numbers in standard form.
   a 0.072 **[1]**
   b 238.9×10^3 **[1]**

2 Write these numbers as ordinary numbers.
   a 9.14×10^6 **[1]**
   b 5.18×10^{-4} **[1]**

3 Which has the greater value, 167.8×10^{-3} or 17×10^{-2}? **[2]**

Look out for

Numbers that are neither an ordinary number nor a number in standard form, e.g. 238.9×10^3

Exam tip

Make sure that numbers are written in the same format, standard form or as ordinary numbers, before comparing.

CHECKED ANSWERS

Calculating with standard form

Rules

When adding or subtracting numbers in standard form, either **1a** make sure that the powers of 10 are the same or **1b** change them into ordinary numbers.

2 When multiplying or dividing numbers in standard form, work with the numbers and the powers of 10 separately.

3 Use the rules of indices: $10^n \times 10^m = 10^{n+m}$ and $10^p \div 10^q = 10^{p-q}$.

Worked examples

a Work out

i $(2.38 \times 10^5) + (5.37 \times 10^3)$ **ii** $(4.45 \times 10^3) \times (7.16 \times 10^{-2})$

giving your answers in standard form.

Answers

i $2.38 \times 10^5 + 5.37 \times 10^3$ **OR** $2.38 \times 10^5 + 5.37 \times 10^3$
1a $= 238 \times 10^3 + 5.37 \times 10^3$ **1b** $= 238\,000 + 5370$
$= (238 + 5.37) \times 10^3$ $= 243\,370$
$= 243.37 \times 10^3$ $= 2.4337 \times 10^5$
$= 2.4337 \times 10^5$

ii $4.45 \times 10^3 \times 7.16 \times 10^{-2}$
2 $= 4.45 \times 7.16 \times 10^3 \times 10^{-2}$
$= 31.862 \times 10^1$ **3**
$= 3.1862 \times 10 \times 10^1$
$= 3.1862 \times 10^2$

b How many times greater than 9.27×10^3 is 3.16×10^8?

Answer
Number of times is $(3.16 \times 10^8) \div (9.27 \times 10^3)$

$= 3.16 \div 9.27 \times 10^8 \div 10^3$ **2**
$= 0.340\,88... \times 10^5$ **3**
$= 3.4088... \times 10^{-1} \times 10^5$ **2**
$= 3.4088... \times 10^4$

Key terms

Standard form

Ordinary number

Powers, indices

Exam tip

Give your answer in standard form if the question asks for it.

Look out for

Be careful not to write:

$3.16 \div 9.27 \times 10^8 \times 10^3$, the powers in 10 also need to be divided.

Exam-style questions

1 $p = 6.32 \times 10^4$ $q = 7.15 \times 10^{-2}$
Work out
a pq **[2]**
b $(p + q)^2$ **[2]**
Give your answers in standard form.

2 The diameter of a water molecule is 2.9×10^{-8} cm. One nanometre $= 1 \times 10^{-9}$ metres.
What is the diameter of this water molecule in nanometres?
Give your answers in standard form. **[2]**

3 One light year $= 9.461 \times 10^{12}$ km.
The average distance from the Sun to Earth $= 1.496 \times 10^8$
How many times greater is one light year than the average distance from the Sun to Earth?
Give your answers in standard form. **[2]**

Exam tip

Do not try to do the whole of each calculation on your calculator. Write down each stage of your working.

CHECKED ANSWERS

Rounding to decimal places, significance and approximating

REVISED

MEDIUM

Rules

1. To round a number to decimal places, look at the next number after the required number of decimal places; **1a** if it is 5 or above, increase the previous place number by 1; **1b** if it is less than 5, do not change the previous place number.
2. To round a number to significant places, count the number of digits from the first non-zero digit, starting from the left then round as above.
3. To estimate the approximate answer to a calculation, round each number to **one** significant figure (1 s.f.).

Worked examples

a Write 4.754
   i correct to 1 decimal place
   ii correct to 3 significant figures.

   Answers
   1 i   4.754 = 4.8
   2 ii 4.754 = 4.75

b Write 0.01278
   i correct to 2 decimal places,
   ii correct to 2 significant figures.

   Answers
   1 i   0.01278 = 0.01
   2 ii 0.01278 = 0.013

c Write down an estimate for the value of
   i 1026
   ii 0.498

   Answers
   3 i   1026 = 1000
      ii 0.498 = 0.5

1a the next number after the required number of decimal places

2a the next number after the required number of significant figures

1b the next number after the required number of decimal places

2b the next number after the required number of significant figures

Key terms

Decimal places

Significant figures

Approximation

Estimate

Look out for

When identifying significant figures, remember the first two 0s here are not significant; the number 1 is the first significant figure.

Exam tip

The size of the number does not change.

Look out for

A common mistake is to write 0.498 = 0

Exam-style questions

1 The dimensions of a rectangle are 4.87 cm × 2.35 cm.
   Work out the area of this rectangle.
   Give your answer correct to 2 decimal places. **[2]**

2 The length of a piece of string is given as 12 cm correct to 2 significant figures.
   Write down the least possible actual length of this piece of string. **[1]**

3 Find an estimate for the value of $\frac{4.83 \times 204}{0.51}$ **[2]**

Exam tip

Round each number correct to **one** significant figure.

CHECKED ANSWERS

Limits of accuracy

HIGH

Rules

1. Given a degree of accuracy for a number, to find a lower bound, write down the midpoint of the given number and the number with one degree of accuracy less.
2. Given a degree of accuracy for a number, to find an upper bound, write down the midpoint of the given number and the number with one degree of accuracy more.

Worked examples

a The length of a football pitch is measured as 120 yards to the nearest yard.

Write down the
i   lower bound
ii upper bound of this length.

Answers

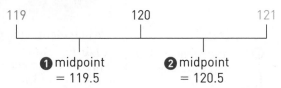

i   lower bound = 119.5 yards
ii upper bound = 120.5 yards

b The volume of a bottle is 85 cm³ correct to the nearest 5 cm³. Write down the **i** lower bound and **ii** upper bound of this volume.

Answers

i   lower bound = 82.5 cm³
ii upper bound = 87.5 cm³

Key terms

Upper bound

Lower bound

Degree of accuracy

Exam tip

Draw a diagram to show the numbers below and above that given.

Look out for

5 cm³ is the degree of accuracy, so the scale must go 5 cm³ below and 5 cm³ above.

Remember

The upper bounds are boundaries, not values that the quantity could actually equal; so do **not** write, 120.49... or 87.49... in i and ii.

Exam-style questions

1 The dimensions of the top of a table are given as 2.3 m × 1.2 m measured correct to 1 decimal place. Write down the
   a lower bound
   b upper bound of these dimensions. **[2]**

2 Mo runs a distance of 2.5 km measured correct to the nearest 10 metres. Find the lower bound of Mo's run. **[1]**

3 The distance of Milly's house to her grandfather's house is 190 miles measured to the nearest 10 miles. It took Milly **exactly** three hours to drive to her grandfather's house. Milly says 'my average speed was 60 mph'. Could Milly be right? Explain your answer. **[3]**

Exam tip

Remember: speed = $\dfrac{\text{distance}}{\text{time}}$

CHECKED ANSWERS

Multiplying and dividing fractions

Rules

1. When multiplying fractions, multiply the numerators together and multiply the denominators together.
2. When dividing fractions, invert the fraction (turn the fraction upside down) that you are dividing by, then multiply the fractions together using Rule ❶.
3. Always simplify your answer by cancelling.

Worked examples

a Work out

  i $\frac{2}{3} \times \frac{5}{7}$

  ii $\frac{1}{4} \times \frac{3}{5} \times \frac{2}{9}$

Answers

  i ❶ $\frac{2}{3} \times \frac{5}{7} = \frac{2 \times 5}{3 \times 7} = \frac{10}{21}$

  ii ❶ $\frac{1}{4} \times \frac{3}{5} \times \frac{2}{9} = \frac{1 \times 3 \times 2}{4 \times 5 \times 9} = \frac{6}{180}$

  ❸ simplifying $\frac{6}{180}$ gives $\frac{1}{30}$

b Work out

  i $\frac{5}{9} \div \frac{1}{3}$ ii $\frac{21}{40} \div \frac{24}{35}$

Give your answers in their simplest form.

Answers

  i $\frac{5}{9} \div \frac{1}{3} = \frac{5}{9} \times \frac{3}{1} = \frac{15}{9} = \frac{5}{3}$

  $\qquad\quad$ ❷ $\quad$ ❶ $\quad$ ❸

  ii $\frac{21}{40} \div \frac{35}{24} = \frac{\overset{3}{\cancel{21}}}{\underset{5}{\cancel{40}}} \times \frac{\overset{3}{\cancel{24}}}{\underset{5}{\cancel{35}}}$ ❷ $= \frac{3 \times 3}{5 \times 5}$ ❶ $= \frac{9}{25}$

> **Exam tip**
>
> If 'giving your answer in its simplest form' is not asked for $\frac{6}{180}$ would get full marks.

> **Key terms**
>
> Numerator
> Denominator
> Product
> Quotient

> **Exam tip**
>
> It is sometimes easier to cancel numbers in the numerator with numbers in the denominator before multiplying out.

Exam-style questions

1 Work out

  a $\frac{3}{10} \times \frac{7}{12} \times \frac{5}{42}$ **[2]**

  b $\frac{12}{9} \div \frac{18}{30}$ **[2]**

2 Mike, Ali and Emily share some money. Mike has $\frac{2}{3}$ of the money.
  Ali has one quarter of the amount that Mike has.
  Emily has the rest of the money.
  a What fraction of the money does Ali have? **[2]**
  Mike's share is divided into 5 equal parts.
  b What fraction of the original sum of money are each of these parts? **[2]**

> **Exam tip**
>
> Dividing by 5 is the same as dividing by $\frac{5}{1}$

CHECKED ANSWERS

Adding and subtracting fractions and working with mixed numbers

Rules

1. When adding or subtracting fractions, find equivalent fractions so that all denominators are the same number.
2. Given a mixed number, to convert to a top-heavy or improper fraction, multiply the whole number by the denominator and add the numerator. This gives the new numerator.
3. Given a top-heavy (improper) fraction, to convert to a mixed number, divide the numerator by the denominator to get the whole number. The remainder is then the new numerator of the fraction part of the mixed number.

Worked examples

a Work out

i $\frac{2}{5} + \frac{1}{6}$

ii $\frac{7}{8} - \frac{3}{7}$

Answers

i $\frac{2}{5} + \frac{1}{6} = \frac{12}{30} + \frac{5}{30}$ ❶ $= \frac{17}{30}$

ii $\frac{7}{8} - \frac{3}{7} = \frac{49}{56} - \frac{24}{56}$ ❶ $= \frac{25}{56}$

b **i** Work out $\frac{2}{3} + \frac{3}{4} - \frac{1}{5}$

ii Work out $2\frac{2}{3} \times 3\frac{3}{4}$

Give your answers as mixed numbers.

Answers

i $\frac{2}{3} + \frac{3}{4} - \frac{1}{5} = \frac{40}{60} + \frac{45}{60} - \frac{12}{60}$ ❶ $= \frac{73}{60} = 1\frac{13}{60}$

❸ 73 ÷ 60 = 1 remainder 13

ii $2 \times 3 = 6 \qquad 6 + 2 = 8$

$2\frac{2}{3} \times 3\frac{3}{4} = \frac{8}{3} \times \frac{15}{4} = \frac{120}{12} = 10$
(❷ ❷ ❸)

Look out for

Do **not** try to add or subtract fractions if the denominators are different

Key terms

Numerator

Denominator

Improper fraction

Top-heavy fraction

Mixed number

Exam tip

To find a common denominator, find the LCM (prime factorisation) of all denominators.

Exam-style questions

1 Work out

a $\frac{5}{8} + \frac{1}{3}$ **[2]**

b $5\frac{1}{4} - 2\frac{5}{12}$ **[2]**

2 A bag contains some counters. $\frac{2}{5}$ of the counters are red; $\frac{3}{8}$ of the counters are blue. The rest of the counters are yellow.
   a What fraction are not blue? **[1]**
   b What fraction are yellow? **[2]**

3 Here is a rectangle.
   Work out the area of the rectangle. **[3]**

$5\frac{1}{3}$ metres

$2\frac{1}{8}$ metres

Exam tip

It is often easier to convert to improper fractions instead of considering the whole numbers and fractions separately when adding or subtracting mixed numbers.

CHECKED ANSWERS

Converting fractions and decimals to and from percentages

Rules

❶ To convert a fraction or a decimal to a percentage, multiply the fraction or decimal by 100 and then evaluate.

❷ To convert a percentage to a fraction, write the percentage over 100 and simplify the fraction.

❸ To convert a percentage to a decimal, divide the percentage by 100.

Worked examples

a Convert to %

  i $\frac{3}{8}$

  ii $1\frac{1}{7}$

  iii   0.6

  iv   4.28

Answers

  i $\frac{3}{8} \times 100$ ❶ $= \frac{300}{8} = 300 \div 8 = 37.5\%$

  ii $1\frac{1}{7} \times 100$ ❶ $= \frac{8}{7} \times 100 = \frac{800}{7} = 800 \div 7 = 114.285...\%$ or $114\frac{2}{7}\%$

  iii 0.6×100 ❶ $= 60\%$

  iv 4.28×100 ❶ $= 428\%$

b Convert
  i   8.5%
  ii   240% to a fraction and a decimal.

Answers

  i $8.5\% = \frac{8.5}{100} = \frac{17}{200}$ ❷ ; $8.5\% = 8.5 \div 100 = 0.085$ ❸

  ii $240\% = \frac{240}{100} = \frac{24}{10} = \frac{12}{5} = 2\frac{2}{5}$ ❷ ; $240\% = 240 \div 100 = 2.40$ ❸

Remember

Percentage means **out of 100**

Key term

Percentage

Look out for

Percentages can also be over 100

Exam tip

Always write down the method; either multiplying by 100 or dividing by 100

Exam-style questions

1 Write the following in order of size.

  20% $\frac{2}{9}$ 0.21 $\frac{1}{4}$ 0.202

  Start with the smallest value. **[2]**

2 Work out the difference between 85% and $\frac{9}{11}$.

  Give your answer as a decimal. **[2]**

3 There are some pencil crayons in a box. 20% of the crayons are red; $\frac{3}{8}$ of the crayons are blue. The rest of the crayons are either green or yellow. There are the same number of green crayons as yellow crayons.

  What percentage of yellow crayons are there in the box? **[3]**

Exam tip

It is best to convert all numbers to decimals or percentages; never convert to fractions.

Applying percentage increases and decreases to amounts

Rules

1a Find the actual increase by finding the percentage of the given amount, then add this value to the original amount.

1b A multiplier can be found by adding the percentage increase to 100 then dividing by 100. The increased amount is then found by applying this multiplier.

2a Find the actual decrease by finding the percentage of the given amount, then subtract this value from the original amount.

2b A multiplier can be found by subtracting the percentage decrease from 100 then dividing by 100. The reduced amount is then found by applying this multiplier.

MEDIUM

Key terms

Percentage

Increase

Decrease

Multiplier

Worked examples

a Increase £250 by 12%

Answer

Method 1
1a 12% of 250 = $\frac{12}{100} \times 250 = 30$

$250 + 30 = £280$

Method 2
1b Multiplier = $\frac{100+12}{100} = \frac{112}{100} = 1.12$

$250 \times 1.12 = £280$

b In a sale the cost of a coat is reduced by 35%. Work out the sale price of the coat if it originally cost £79

Answer

Method 1
2a 35% of £78.50 = $\frac{35}{100} \times 79 = 27.65$

$79 - 27.65 = £51.35$

Method 2
2a Multiplier = $\frac{100-35}{100} = \frac{65}{100} = 0.65$

$79 \times 0.65 = £51.35$

Exam tip

When using multipliers, show how they are found.

Exam-style questions

1 A ball of string has 8.5 metres in length of string. A piece of string is cut from this ball. The piece of string is 1.5% of the length of string on the ball. Work out the length of this piece of string. Give your answer in centimetres. **[2]**

2 Peter buys a painting for £360. If he sells the painting in an auction he is likely to make a 12.5% profit. Peter sells the painting privately for £400. Could Peter have made a greater profit if he had sold the painting at the auction? **[4]**

3 There are 48 red and 60 white counters in a bag. $33\frac{1}{3}\%$ of the red counters are removed. The number of white counters is increased by 20%. Are there more or less counters now in the bag? **[4]**

Exam tip

Work in consistent units (cm here).

Exam tip

Show clearly each part of your methods.

Look out for

A common mistake is to decrease when you should be increasing a value (and vice versa).

CHECKED ANSWERS

Finding the percentage change from one amount to another

Rules

❶ To find one quantity as a percentage of another, write the quantity as a fraction of the other and multiply by 100.

❷ To find percentage change, write the change from the original amount as a fraction and then multiply by 100.

Key term

Percentage

Worked examples

a Find 2.4 as a percentage of 15.

Simplify by cancelling.

Answer

$\frac{2.4}{15} \times 100$ ❶ $= \frac{240}{15} = \frac{48}{3} = 16\%$

b The average speed of a train increased from 208 mph to 234 mph. Work out the percentage change.

Answer

234 − 208 = 26

% change $= \frac{26}{208} \times 100$ = ❷ $\frac{2600}{208}$ = 12.5% increase.

Exam tips

On a calculator paper use your calculator but write down what calculations you are doing.

On a non-calculator paper fractions will usually cancel.

Exam-style questions

1 Work out 65p as a percentage of £26 **[2]**

2 At the start of summer, Sam weighed 80 kg. Over the summer, Sam's weight increased by 2.5%. Sam then went on a diet and has now lost 5 kg in weight.

   Work out the percentage change in Sam's weight from the start of summer to now. **[4]**

3 Nazia and Debra are market traders. Nazia paid £428 for some goods and sold them for £492.20. Debra paid £296 for some goods and sold them for £338.92.

   Who made the greater percentage profit? **[4]**

Exam tip

Always state if increase or decrease.

Exam tip

You must always explain your answer. An answer of 'Nazia' or 'Debra' gets no credit.

CHECKED ANSWERS

Reverse percentages

Rules

❶ If the final value is the result of a percentage increase, add 100% to the percentage increase and divide the final value by this new percentage.

❷ If the final value is the result of a percentage decrease, subtract the percentage decrease from 100% and divide the final value by this new percentage.

Worked examples

a In a sale the price of a TV is reduced by 15%.
If the sale price is £544, work out the original price of the TV.

Answer
The price is a reduction so: 100% − 15% = 85% (which is $\frac{85}{100}$).

❷ $544 \div \frac{85}{100} = 544 \times \frac{100}{85} = £640$

b N is increased by 80%. Its value is now 126.
What was the value of N?

Answer
This is an increase so: 100% + 80% = 180% (which is $\frac{180}{100} = 1.8$)

N = 126 ÷ 1.8 = 70

Key terms

Percentage increase

Percentage decrease

Remember

To divide by a fraction, invert the fraction then multiply by it.

This is the multiplier of the increase

Exam tip

If using a multiplier, show how you get it.

Exam-style questions

1 Ismail bought a smart phone and a laptop. The total cost, including VAT at a rate of 20%, was £684. The price of the smart phone excluding VAT was £250.

What was the price of the laptop excluding VAT? **[3]**

2 David keeps bees. In 2015 he had 6400 bees. This was an increase of 27.5% on 2014.

David said he had less than 5000 bees in 2014. Is David right? **[3]**

3 Ben has changed his job. His new salary is 5% less than before. Ben's wife Jane has just had an 8% increase in her salary. Ben's salary is now £26 500 per year. Jane's salary is now £22 000 per year.

Are their total earnings better or worse now? **[4]**

Look out for

Be clear if the answer is going to be greater than or less than the original value.

Look out for

A common mistake is to find the percentage of the final amount and subtract or add depending upon whether the original value will be less or greater.

CHECKED ANSWERS

Repeated percentage increase/decrease

Rules

1. Find the increase (decrease) after one period of time and add (subtract) this to the original amount. The percentage increase (decrease) is then applied to this total amount and a new total found. This continues for the required number of repetitions.
2. If an increase or decrease in percentage is repeated n times, the compounded value can be found using the multiplier raised to the power of n.

Key term

Compound interest

Worked examples

a Tim invests £4000 in a savings account. Compound interest is paid at a rate of 3.5% per annum. How much will Tim have in his account after 4 years?

Answer

1 3.5% of $4000 = \frac{3.5}{100} \times 4000 = 140$

Total after 1 year = 4000 + 140 = 4140

1 3.5% of $4140 = \frac{3.5}{100} \times 4140 = 144.90$

Total after 2 years = 4140 + 144.90 = 4284.90

1 3.5% of $4284.90 = \frac{3.5}{100} \times 4284.90 = 149.97$

Total after 3 years = 4284.90 + 149.97 = 4434.87

1 3.5% of $4434.87 = \frac{3.5}{100} \times 4434.87 = 155.22$

Total after 4 years = 4434.87 + 155.22 = 4590.09

2 Multiplier = $\frac{100 + 3.5}{100} = 1.035$

$n = 4$ since it is a 4-year period

Total after 4 years = $4000 \times 1.035^4 = 4590.09$

Exam tip

1.035^4 is found using the y^x button on the calculator. Some calculators do not have a y^x.

Exam tip

Method 2 is clearly a more direct method.

b The population of birds in a bird sanctuary is 4500. It is estimated that the population will decrease at a rate of 12% each year for the next 3 years. What is the expected population after the next 3 years?

Answer

Multiplier = $\frac{100 - 12}{100} = 0.88$

2 Expected population = $4500 \times 0.88^3 = 3066$

Look out for

Be clear if the answer is going to be greater than or less than the original value.

Exam-style questions

1 A bank pays interest at a rate of 4.5% for the first year and 2% for each subsequent year. Tess invests £35 000 for 5 years. Work out the total interest paid at the end of 5 years. **[3]**

2 Chris bought a new car for £17 500. It is estimated that the car will depreciate in value by 20% in the first year, 15% in the second year and 12% pa for the next 3 years. Chris says that after 5 years the value of the car will be greater than half the cost of the car. Is Chris right? **[4]**

3 Jose has just opened a new restaurant. He predicts that his profits will increase by 12.5% every 6 months. How many years will have passed before Jose's profits are double what they were after the first 6-month period? **[3]**

Exam tip

Use multipliers wherever possible in this exercise.

CHECKED ANSWERS

Mixed exam-style questions

1   Paul says $5 \times 2 + 3 - 7$ is equal to 18.
    Lisa says $5 \times 2 + 3 - 7$ is equal to 6.
    By inserting a pair of brackets, show that both Paul and Lisa could be right.   [2]

2   Naomi is paid £8.45 per hour for a 35 hour week.
    She works 12 hours overtime at a rate of £12.60 per hour.
    Izmail says 'If I work for 45 hours at £9.80 per hour, I will earn more than Naomi.'
    Is Izmail right?   [4]

3   Sweets are sold in tubes and in boxes.
    A tube contains 40 sweets and costs 48p.
    A box contains 112 sweets and costs £1.40
    a   Which offers the better value for money, a tube or a box of sweets?   [3]
    b   Mary needs 180 sweets to decorate a cake.
        What is the most economical way of buying enough sweets?   [2]

4   Given that $27.3 \times 5.9 = 161.07$, work out
    a 0.0273×59 [1]
    b 27.3×5.8 [2]

5   Write these numbers in order of size, smallest first.
    2.56×10^3 255×10^{-1} $25 \div 10^{-2}$ 26×10^2 0.0026×10^5 [2]

6   The diagram shows a right-angled triangle.
    a   Write the dimensions correct to 1 decimal place then work
        out the area of the triangle.   [3]
    b   If the dimensions were written correct to 2 decimal places,
        would the area of the triangle be greater than your answer
        in **a** or less? Explain your answer. Do not work out the
        actual area to answer this.   [1]

    7.564 cm
    3.958 cm

7   The length of a rectangle is 8.364 cm. The width of the rectangle is 5.549 cm.
    Tony says that the area of the rectangle is least when the length and width are rounded to
    1 significant figure.
    Noreen says it is least when the length and width are rounded to 2 significant figures.
    Waqar says it is least when the length and width are rounded to 3 significant figures.
    Who is right?   [4]

8   In a cinema there are 29 rows of seats with 41 seats in each row.
    The cost of a ticket for this cinema is £5.95.
    Last night every seat in the cinema was taken.
    Estimate the total cost of the tickets for last night.   [3]

9   Saturn is 1.25×10^9 km from Earth. Venus is 4.14×10^7 km from Earth.
    a   How many times is Saturn further from Earth than Venus?   [2]
    b   How many miles is Saturn from Earth?   [2]

10 The dimensions of a rectangular piece of paper are given as $30 \text{ cm} \times 18 \text{ cm}$ measured
    correct to the nearest centimetre.
    Could the area of this piece of paper be greater than 550 cm^2? Explain your answer.   [3]

Sharing in a given ratio

Rules

❶ To share an amount in the ratio $a : b : c$, find the value of one unit of the amount, divide the amount by the sum of a, b and c.

❷ Then multiply this answer by each of a, b and c.

❸ To find the fraction of each part of the ratio $a : b : c$, write each part as a fraction out of the sum of a, b and c.

Worked examples

a Tom, Mary and Sally share £72 in the ratio 4 : 3 : 2. Work out how much each person gets.

Answer

❶ $72 \div (4 + 3 + 2) = 72 \div 9 = £8$ per share

❷ Tom gets £8 × 4 = £32,
Mary gets £8 × 3 = £24,
Sally gets £8 × 2 = £16

b The ratio of a mixture of cement and sand is 1 : 4. What fraction of the mixture is
i cement
ii sand?

Answers

❸ **i** cement = $\frac{1}{1+4} = \frac{1}{5}$

ii sand = $\frac{4}{1+4} = \frac{4}{5}$

Key terms

Ratio

Proportion

Look out for

A common mistake is to write $\frac{1}{4}$ for the fraction of cement.

Exam-style questions

1 Divide £132 in the ratio 5 : 4 : 2 **[2]**

2 In an election, the ratio of Conservative voters to Labour voters to other voters is 9 : 5 : 3. 27 132 people voted in this election.

How many more people voted Conservative than Labour? **[3]**

3 A shop sells coffee in three different sizes of packet. The volume of coffee in each packet is in the ratio 3 : 4 : 5. The cost of each size of packet is £4.30, £6.30 and £7.50.

Which size of packet gives the best value for money? **[4]**

Exam tips

Always work out the value of **one** share.

Always check that your answers add up to the amount given.

Exam tip

Make sure your choice is supported by clear working.

CHECKED ANSWERS

Working with proportional quantities

Rules

❶ To use the unitary method, find out what proportion is just **one** part of the whole amount,

❷ Then multiples of that can be found.

Key terms

Ratio

Proportion

Multiples

Worked examples

a 12 identical books cost £23.88.
Work out the cost of 5 of these books.

Answer
❶ 23.88 ÷ 12 = £1.99 per book ◄─────────── The value of **one** unit.
❷ 5 books cost £1.99 × 5 = £9.95

b Work out which is the better value for these bags of potatoes;
6 kg for £8.16 or 11 kg for £15.18.

Answer
❶ £8.16 ÷ 6 = £1.36 per kg

❶ £15.18 ÷ 11 = £1.38 per kg

So 6 kg for £8.16 is the better value.

Exam tip

Always give answers in a sentence supported by working.

Exam-style questions

1 8 pens cost £5.20.

Work out the cost of 15 of these pens. **[2]**

Exam tip

Always work out the value of **one** part.

2 Jay buys three portions of chips and two pies for £6.45. Mandy buys five pies for £6.

How much does one portion of chips cost? **[3]**

Exam tip

Explain why this is the greatest number.

3 Here are the ingredients to make 40 biscuits.
600 g of butter, 300 g of sugar and 900 g of flour.
Mrs Bee has the following ingredients in her cupboard.
1.5 kg of butter, 1 kg of sugar and 2 kg of flour.

Work out the greatest number of these biscuits that Mrs Bee can make. **[4]**

CHECKED ANSWERS

The constant of proportionality

Rules

❶ To work out a constant of proportionality of two variables which are in direct proportion, divide one variable by the other.
❷ To derive a formula describing the relationship between two variables, find the constant of proportionality and then substitute into the relationship.

Worked examples

a The table of values shows the miles (D) travelled by a car using G gallons of petrol.

D miles	120	240	48	72	120
G gallons	5	10	20	30	50

Write down a formula connecting D and G.

Answer
$D \propto G$, so $D = kG$ where k is the constant of proportionality.
❶ $120 \div 5 = 24$; $240 \div 10 = 24$; $480 \div 20 = 24$; $720 \div 30 = 24$; $1200 \div 05 = 24$
$k = 24$ is the constant of proportionality.
❷ $D = 24G$

b y is directly proportional to x.
When $x = 5$, $y = 11$.
Work out the value of x when $y = 30$.
Give your answer correct to 1 decimal place.

Answer
$y \propto x$, so $y = kx$

When $x = 5$, $y = 11$, so $11 = k \times 5$

$k = 11 \div 5 = 2.2$ ❶

$y = 2.2x$ ❷

When $y = 30$, $30 = 2.2x$

$x = 30 \div 2.2 = 13.6$

Exam tip
Remember: '$\propto$' means 'is proportional to'

Key terms
Direct proportion
Constant of proportionality

Exam tip
Step 1: use given information to find k.

Step 2: use value of k to write down formula.

Step 3: use formula to find the required unknown.

Exam-style questions

1 The table of values shows amounts of money in pounds (£P) and their equivalent values in euros (€E)

Pounds (£P)	2.00		6.00		10.00
Euros (€E)	2.70	5.40		10.80	13.50

a Write down the missing figures from the table. **[1]**
b Write down a formula for E in terms of P. **[2]**
c What does the constant of proportionality represent in this formula? **[1]**

2 H is directly proportional to t.
When $t = 5.6$, $H = 14$
Work out the value of H when $t = 35$ **[3]**

CHECKED ANSWERS

Number   21

Working with inversely proportional quantities

Rules

❶ To work out a constant of proportionality of two variables which are inversely proportional to each other, multiply one variable by the other.

❷ To derive a formula describing the relationship between two variables, find the constant of proportionality and then substitute into the relationship.

Worked examples

a A sum of money is divided equally between N people so that each person gets £p.

  i If 30 people each get £25, write down a formula for N in terms of p.

  ii What does the constant of proportionality represent?

Answers

i N is inversely proportional to p, so $N = \frac{k}{p}$

  ❶ $k = 30 \times 25 = 750$, so $N = \frac{750}{p}$ ❷

ii The constant of proportionality, 750, is the amount of money shared.

b W is inversely proportional to d. When $d = 5$, $W = 120$. Work out the value of d when $W = 600$.

Answer

$W \propto \frac{1}{d}$, so $W = \frac{k}{d}$, when $d = 5$, $W = 120$, so $120 = k \div 5$

$k = 120 \times 5 = 600$ ❶

$W = \frac{600}{d}$

When $W = 600$, $600 = 600 \div d$

$d = 600 \div 600 = 1$

Exam tip

Remember:
'$\propto$' means 'is proportional to'
'inverse' means '1 over' or 'reciprocal'

Key terms

Inverse proportion

Constant of proportionality

Exam tip

Step 1: use given information to find k.

Step 2: use value of k to write down formula.

Step 3: use formula to find the required unknown.

Note: this is the **same** process as for direct proportion.

Exam-style questions

1 It takes 8 men 25 days to build a wall. It takes 10 men 20 days to build an identical wall.
  a Is this an example of direct or inverse proportion? You must explain your answer. **[1]**
  b How many days would it take 4 men to build the wall? **[2]**
  (Note: All of the men work at the same rate.)

2 y is inversely proportional to x. The table of values has just one error. What is it? **[2]**

x	1.2	1.5	25	30	120
y	250	200	120	10	2.5

3 P is inversely proportional to s.
When $s = 20$, $P = 100$. Work out the value of s when $P = 200$ **[2]**

CHECKED ANSWERS

Index notation and rules of indices

Rules

1. $a \times a \times a \times \ldots \times a$ (m times) is written a^m.
2. To multiply numbers written in index form, add the powers together. $a^m \times a^n = a^{m+n}$
3. To divide numbers written in index form, subtract the powers. $a^m \div a^n = a^{m-n}$
4. To raise a number written in index form to a given power, multiply the powers together. $(a^m)^n = a^{mn}$

Key terms

Index

Indices

Powers

Worked examples

a   Write $7 \times 7 \times 7 \times 7 \times 7$ in index form.

Answer

1. $7 \times 7 \times 7 \times 7 \times 7 = 7^5$

b   Write $\left(\frac{2^3 \times 2^4}{2^5}\right)^3$ as a power of 2.

Answer

$\left(\frac{2^3 \times 2^4}{2^5}\right)^3 = \left(\frac{2^7}{2^5}\right)^3$ since $2^3 \times 2^4 = 2^{3+4} = 2^7$ 2

$= (2^2)^3$ since $2^7 \div 2^5 = 2^{7-5} = 2^2$ 3

$= 2^6$ since $(2^2)^3 = 2^{2 \times 3} = 2^6$ 4

Exam tip

A common mistake is to multiply powers instead of adding in a product.

Exam tip

A common mistake is to divide powers instead of subtracting in a quotient.

Look out for

Follow the rules of BIDMAS and work out the calculation inside the brackets first.

Exam-style questions

1 a   Write $10 \times 10 \times 10 \times 10$ in index notation. **[1]**
   b   Use your calculator to work out the value of 8^5. **[1]**

2 $x = 8 \times 2^4$ $y = 4^2 \times 16$
   Work out the value of xy. Give your answer as a power of 2 **[3]**

3 Tom is trying to work out the value of $\frac{10^4 \times 10^5}{10 \times 10^2}$

   Tom writes $\frac{10^4 \times 10^5}{10 \times 10^2} = \frac{10^{20}}{10^2} = 10^{10} = 100$.

   Write down each of the mistakes that Tom has made. **[4]**

CHECKED ANSWERS

Prime factorisation

Rules

To write a number as a product of its prime factors, use either the factor-tree method or the method of repeated division.

1 Factor tree method: continue to write each number as a product of two factors until all of the factors are prime numbers; then write these as a product.

2 Repeated division method: Continue to divide by a prime number until the final answer is 1; then write as a product all of the prime numbers that have been used.

3 To find the HCF of numbers written as products of their prime factors, choose all common factors and multiply together.

4 To find the LCM of numbers written as products of their prime factors, choose all factors (common factors just once) and multiply together.

Key term

Prime factors

Worked examples

a Write 108 as a product of its prime factors.

Answer

1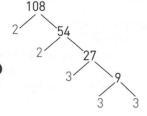

2

2	108
2	54
3	27
3	9
3	3
	1

$108 = 2 \times 2 \times 3 \times 3 \times 3$

$108 = 2 \times 2 \times 3 \times 3 \times 3$

Exam tip

This answer can also be written in index notation as $2^2 \times 3^3$

b Find **i** the HCF of 108 and 80 **ii** the LCM of 108 and 80

Answers

108 written as a product of its prime factors is $2 \times 2 \times \mathbf{3} \times \mathbf{3} \times \mathbf{3}$

80 written as a product of its prime factors is $2 \times 2 \times \mathbf{2} \times \mathbf{2} \times \mathbf{5}$ using **1** or **2**.

i the HCF of 108 and 80 = $2 \times 2 = 4$ **3** choosing common prime factors.

ii the LCM of 108 and 80 = $2 \times 2 \times 3 \times 3 \times 3 \times 2 \times 2 \times 5 = 2160$ **4** choosing all prime factors but writing common factors once only.

Look out for

A common mistake is to list the prime factors without writing as a product: 2, 2, 3, 3, 3 would lose marks.

Exam tip

The LCM is simply the HCF multiplied by all other factors.

Exam-style questions

1 **a** Write 96 as a product of its prime factors. **[2]**
  b Find **i** the HCF of 96 and 120 **ii** the LCM of 96 and 120 **[3]**

2 Nadir is in hospital. She has an injection every 6 hours. She has tablets every 8 hours. She has her bandages changed every 10 hours.
On Monday at 8.00 am Nadir is given an injection, she takes her tablets and has her bandages changed.

When will all three treatments be given to her next at the same time? **[3]**

Mixed exam-style questions

1 $\frac{5}{6}$ of the members of a sports club are male. $\frac{1}{4}$ of the male members are under 18 years of age. $\frac{1}{3}$ of the female members attend keep fit classes.

   a What fraction of the members of the sports club are male and over 18? **[2]**

   b What fraction of the members of the sports club are female and do not attend keep fit classes? **[2]**

2 The table shows the time spent by Helen doing homework last week.

Day	Mon	Tues	Wed	Thurs	Fri
Time in hours	$1\frac{3}{4}$	$2\frac{1}{2}$	$1\frac{1}{3}$	$3\frac{2}{7}$	$\frac{3}{4}$

$\frac{1}{3}$ of her time spent doing homework was in either Maths or English.

Work out the number of hours spent doing either Maths or English. Give your answer as a mixed number. **[3]**

3 Rachel's annual salary is £34 500. Peter's annual salary is £32 900.
Rachel gets a 4% increase in her salary.
Peter gets a 6% increase in his salary.
Whose annual salary is now the greater? **[3]**

4 In 2010, Jason had 5800 stamps in his collection.
In 2011, Jason sold some stamps and reduced his collection by 15%.
In 2012, Jason sold some more stamps reducing his collection by a further 10%.

   a In 2011 and 2012, how many stamps did Jason sell altogether? **[3]**

   b What was the overall percentage reduction in Jason's collection of stamps? **[2]**

5 Brian spends $\frac{2}{5}$ of his monthly earnings on clothes and entertainment.

The ratio of money spent on clothes to money spent on entertainment is $4:3$.
What fraction of his monthly earnings does Brian spend on entertainment? **[3]**

6 Concrete is made from sand, stone and cement.
Bill makes 10 cubic metres of concrete with the ratio of sand, stone and cement equal to $4:3:1$.
Sandra makes 8 cubic metres of concrete with the ratio of sand, stone and cement equal to $6:5:2$.

   a Who uses the most cement, Bill or Sandra? **[3]**

   b If Bill mixed his concrete with sand, stone and cement in the ratio $10:7:2$, how would this affect the amount of cement that he would need? **[1]**

7 Milk is sold in three sizes of bottle, small, medium and large.
A small bottle holds 1 pint of milk and costs £1.24.
A medium bottle holds 1 litre of milk and costs £2.15.
A large bottle holds 1 gallon of milk and costs £9.80.
Which size bottle of milk is the better buy? (1 pint = 0.568 litres) **[4]**

8 From Monday, the price of a TV was reduced by 20% in a sale.
   On Wednesday the TV was reduced by a further 10%.
   Alan bought the TV on Wednesday for £604.80.
   What was the price of the TV before the sale?   [4]

9 y is directly proportional to x and x is directly proportional to z.
   a Prove that y is directly proportional to z.   [2]
   b When $z = 8$, $x = 40$ and $y = 160$. Work out the value of y when $z = 2.5$.   [2]

10 W is inversely proportional to t.
   a W is directly proportional to s. Write down the relationship between t and s.   [1]
   b $W = 8s$ and $t = 10$ when $W = 4$. Find the value of t when $s = 1.5$.   [3]

11 $2^3 \times 2^{2x-1} = 8^{-1}$. Find the value of x.   [3]

12 Find the difference between the LCM and the HCF of 90 and 84.   [4]

Algebra: pre-revision check

Check how well you know each topic by answering these questions. If you get a question wrong, go to the page number in brackets to revise that topic.

1 This formula gives the value of p in terms of q and r.

$p = 2q - 3r$.

Find the value of p when $q = 10$ and $r = 4$.   (page 29)

2 Solve the equations

  a $a + 4 = 6$

  b $\frac{b}{3} = 5$

  c $5c + 4 = 6$

  d $15 - \frac{3e}{2} = 24$ (page 30)

3 a Expand these brackets

    i $5(2a + 3)$

    ii $h(3h - 6)$

    iii $3x(4x - 2y)$

  b Factorise fully

    i $6y + 12$

    ii $6p^2 - 9p$

    iii $5e^2 + 10ef$

    iv $8x^2y - 12xy^2$ (page 31)

4 Solve these equations

  a $5x - 6 = 2x + 3$

  b $7 - 2p = 6p + 13$

  c $2 - \frac{3y}{2} = 5 + \frac{5y}{4}$ (page 32)

5 Solve

  a $5(3g - 2) = 35$

  b $4(5h + 7) = 3(2h + 8)$

  c $2(5k + 8) - 6 = 4(2k - 1)$ (page 33)

6 a Simplify

    i $a^4 \times a^6$

    ii $\frac{x^8}{x^5}$

    iii $\frac{12e^6f^7}{8e^9f^5}$

  b Expand and simplify

    i $(t + 2)(t + 5)$

    ii $(v - 7)(v + 5)$

    iii $(y - 6)(y - 5)$ (page 34)

7 This formula is used to find the distance, S, travelled by an object.

$$S = ut + \frac{1}{2}at^2$$

  a Find the value of S when $u = 5$, $t = 4$ and $a = 10$.

  b Make a the subject of the formula.   (page 35)

8 Prove that the sum of the three consecutive numbers $(n - 1)$, n and $(n + 1)$ is a multiple of 3. (page 36)

9 Here are the first 5 terms of a linear sequence.

    4   10   16   22   28

  a Find the nth term of the sequence.

  b Work out the 50th term in the sequence.

  c Explain if 900 is a member of the sequence. (page 37)

10 a Write down the first 5 terms of the quadratic sequence with nth term $2n^2 - 3$.

  b Find the nth term of the quadratic sequence that has the first 5 terms 3, 8, 15, 24, 35. (page 38)

11 The nth term of quadratic sequence is $n^2 + 5$. The nth term of a different quadratic sequence is $80 - 2n^2$.

Find the number that is in both sequences. (page 39)

12 Here is a geometric sequence.

    5   15   45   135   ...

  a Find the common ratio.

  b Find the 10th term of the sequence.   (page 40)

13 a On a coordinate grid drawn with values of x from -3 to $+3$ and values of y from -6 to $+8$, draw the graph of $y = 2x + 1$.

  b Find the value of x when $y = 6$ (page 42)

14 Here is the graph that shows the depth of water in a harbour. A ship needs to enter the harbour between 08:00 and 20:00. It needs a 4 metre depth of water in the harbour. Between what times can the ship enter the harbour?   (page 43)

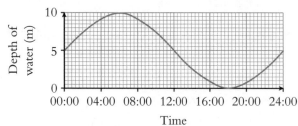

15 Find the equation of a straight line graph that passes through the point (0, −2) and has a gradient of 3.   (page 45)

16 a On a coordinate grid drawn with values of x from −2 to +4 and values of y from −6 to +8, draw the graph of $y = x^2 − 3x − 2$.
b Find the values of x when $x^2 − 3x − 2 = 0$.
(page 46)

17 Find the equation of a straight line graph that passes through the point (−3, 3) and is parallel to the line $x + 2y = 8$.   (page 47)

18 a Sketch the graph of the quadratic function $y = x^2 − 4x + 3$ for values of x from 0 to 5.
b Write down the roots of the equation $x^2 − 4x + 3 = 0$.
c Write down the line of symmetry of the graph.   (page 48)

19 a On a coordinate grid drawn with values of x from −3 to +3 and values of y from −10 to +30, draw the graph of $y = x^3 + x^2 − 3x$.
b Find the values of x when $x^3 + x^2 − 3x = 0$.
(page 49)

20 a Write down the inequality shown on this number line.

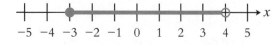

b Solve these inequalities
i $2x + 5 < 9$
ii $24 + 2t > 30 − 3t$
iii $5(y − 3) \leqslant 3y − 6$ (page 50)

21 Solve this pair of simultaneous equations.
$5x + 2y = 8$
$2x − y = 5$ (page 51)

22 Here is the graph of the line $y + 2x = 3$.

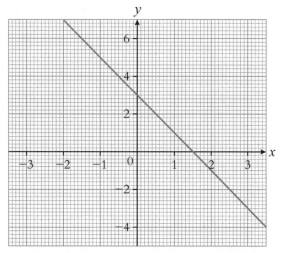

Find graphically the solution to the simultaneous equations:
$y + 2x = 3$
$y − 2x = 1$ (page 52)

23 a Expand and simplify
i $(x + 4)(x − 5)$
ii $(y + 8)(y − 8)$
iii $(6 − a)(a + 6)$
b Factorise
i $x^2 + 7x + 12$
ii $e^2 − 3e − 10$
iii $b^2 − 25$ (page 53)

24 Solve the equations
a $x^2 − 5x + 6 = 0$
b $x^2 − 2x = 15$
c $p^2 − 49 = 0$ (page 54)

Working with formulae

Rules

1. You can replace words or letters in a formula with numbers.
2. Use BIDMAS to find the value of the missing word or letter.
3. Use inverses to write the formula or equation so that the missing letter is on its own on one side of the formula or equation.

Worked examples

a Here is a formula to find the perimeter of a rectangle:
$P = 2l + 2w$.
Find the value of P when $l = 6$ and $w = 4$.

Answer
$P = 2l + 2w$

1 $P = 2 \times 6 + 2 \times 4$

2 $P = 12 + 8 = 20$

b Tom hires a car from Cars 2U.

Cars 2U

i How much does it cost to hire a car for 7 days?

ii Ben has £100.
For how many days can he hire a car?
You must explain your answer.

£20 plus £30 a day

Answers

i Cost = $20 + 7 \times 30$ **1**
Cost = $20 + 210$ **2**
Cost = £230

ii $100 = 20 + N \times 30$ **1**
$100 - 20 = N \times 30$ **3**
$80 = N \times 30$ so $N = 80 \div 30 = 2.666...$ **2**
Ben can hire the car for 2 days.
This costs £80.
3 days cost £110 which is too much.

Look out for

$2w$ means $2 \times w$

So if $w = 5$ then $2w$ is $2 \times 5 = 10$ and not 25

Key terms

Formula

Substitute

Variable

Equation

Exam tips

Always show your working when answering algebra questions.

Do not use trial and error methods as you may well lose marks.

Exam-style questions

1 Bobbie uses this number machine to work out the number of cartons of orange juice she needs for a party.

Number of people ÷5 +2 Number of cartons

   a How many cartons will Bobbie need for 40 people? **[2]**
   b How many people are in a party that uses 20 cartons? **[2]**

2 This formula gives the time taken, T minutes, to cook a chicken of weight w kg.
$T = 40w + 20$
   a How long does it take to cook a chicken of weight 2.5 kg? **[2]**

It takes 3 hours 20 minutes to cook a different chicken.
   b How heavy was the chicken? **[2]**

Setting up and solving simple equations

Rules

1. Always use the inverse operations to solve an equation.
2. + and − are the inverse of one another.
3. × and ÷ are the inverse of one another.
4. To set up an equation a variable must be defined.

Worked examples

a   **2** $2p + 5 = 17$ (−5 is the inverse operation of + 5)

      $2p + 5 − 5 = 17 − 5$ (subtract 5 from each side of the equation)

    3 $2p = 12$ (÷ 2 is the inverse of × 2)

      $p = 6$ (divide each side of the equation by 2)

b   **2**   Ann is two years younger than Ben.
Clara is twice as old as Ben.
The total of their ages is 58.
Work out their ages.

Answer

Let Ben's age be x

Ann's age will be $x − 2$

Clara's age will be $2x$

Firstly, set up the equation:

$x + (x − 2) + 2x = 58$

Now collect like terms:

$4x − 2 = 62$

$4x = 60$ (Add 2 to each side)

$x = 15$ (Divide each side by 4)

Ann will be 13, Ben 15 and Clara 30.

Key terms

Equation

Inverse operation

Solve

Variable

Exam tips

Always use algebraic methods and show your working to gain full marks.

Always check your answer to make sure it is correct.

Exam-style questions

1 Solve the equations

   a $a − 3 = 7$ **[1]**   b $\frac{b}{5} = 3$ **[1]**   c $3c + 9 = 7$ **[2]**

   d $\frac{5d}{2} + 4 = 29$ **[2]**   e $6 − 2e = 3$ **[2]**

2 Here is a rectangle.
The length is $2x + 5$.
The width is $x − 3$.
The perimeter is 46 cm.

$2x + 5$

$x − 3$

Work out the area of the rectangle in cm².   **[4]**

CHECKED ANSWERS

Using brackets

Rules

1. When you expand a bracket you multiply what is inside the bracket by the number or variable outside the bracket.
2. When you factorise an algebraic expression you take out the common factor from each term of the expression and put it outside the bracket.

Worked examples

a Expand

   i $4(3x + 5)$

Answers

$4 \times (3x + 5)$

$4 \times 3x + 4 \times 5$

$12x + 20$

$t \times (3t - 4)$

$t \times 3t - t \times 4$

$3t^2 - 4t$

b Factorise

   i $4p + 6$ **ii** $6p^2q - 9pq^2$

Answers

$2 \times 2 \times p + 2 \times 3$

2 is in 4 and in 6

2 $2(2p + 3)$

$3 \times p \times q \times 2 \times p - 3 \times p \times q \times 3 \times q$

3 and p and q are in both terms

2 $3pq(2p - 3q)$

Look out for

$x \times x = x^2$ using index laws

Key terms

Brackets

Variable

Expression

Expand

Factorise

Exam-style questions

1 Beth is 3 years older than Amy.
Cath is twice as old as Beth.
The total of their ages is 41.
How old are the three girls? **[3]**

2 *PQRS* is a rectangle.
The length of the rectangle is
$(2x - 5)$ cm.
The width of the rectangle is 6 cm.
The area of the rectangle is 72 cm².
Work out the perimeter of the
rectangle. **[4]**

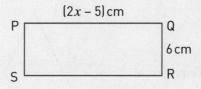

Exam tips

Always check your answer by multiplying out the brackets.

Always define your variable e.g. let Amy's age be x.

Then set up your equation.

CHECKED ANSWERS

Solving equations with the unknown on both sides

Rules

1. Keep the variables on the side of the equation that has the highest number of that variable and move the numbers to the other side of the equation.
2. Then solve the equation.

Worked examples

a   Solve $5x + 4 = 2x - 8$

Answer

$5x - 2x + 4 = -8$ ❶

$3x = -8 - 4$ ❷

$3x = -12$

$x = -4$

b   Solve $5.5 - 2.4y = 1.6y - 2.5$

Answer

$5.5 = 1.6y + 2.4y - 2.5$ ❶

$5.5 + 2.5 = 4y$ ❷

$8 = 4y$

$y = 2$

Look out for

The variable on both sides of the equation.

($5x$ is bigger than $2x$ so keep the xs on the left-hand side of the equation)

($1.6y$ is bigger than $-2.4y$ so keep the ys on the right-hand side of the equation)

Key terms

Variable

Solve

Exam-style questions

1   Here is a rectangle.
All measurements are in cm.

Find the area of the rectangle in cm². **[5]**

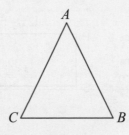

$3r + 4$

$2p + 3$ $4p - 2$

$7r - 8$

Exam tip

Always set up your equations first.

2   Here is a triangle.
Angle $A = 2x + 30$
Angle $B = 5x - 15$
Angle $C = 3x + 15$

Prove that triangle ABC is an equilateral triangle.
What assumptions have you made in your proof? **[5]**

CHECKED ANSWERS

Solving equations with brackets

Rules

❶ Multiply out (expand) the brackets.
❷ Then solve the equation.

Worked examples

a Solve $3(2x + 5) = 27$

Answer

$3 \times 2x + 3 \times 5 = 27$ (Expand the bracket) ❶

$6x + 15 = 27$ ❷

$6x = 12$

$x = 2$

b Solve $5(3y - 2) = 3(6y + 5) - 13$

Answer

$5 \times 3y - 5 \times 2 = 3 \times 6y + 3 \times 5 - 13$ (Expand the brackets) ❶

$15y - 10 = 18y + 15 - 13$ ❷

$15y - 10 = 18y + 2$

$-12 = 3y$

$y = -4$

Look out for

Brackets that will need to be multiplied out.

Key terms

Variable

Expand

Bracket

Solve

(Move the variables to the right-hand side as it is the one with the highest number of the variable)

Exam-style questions

1 Abbi thinks of a number n.
She doubles the number and adds 5.
Abbi then multiplies her answer by 5 and gets 85.
Find the number Abbi first thought of. **[3]**

2 Here is a rectangle
The perimeter of the rectangle
is 210 cm.
Work out the area of the
rectangle. **[3]**

$3(2x + 5)$ cm

$2(2x - 5)$ cm

Exam tips

Always set up your equations first.

CHECKED ANSWERS

Simplifying harder expressions and expanding two brackets

Rules

1. Index law for multiplying numbers or variables raised to a power is
$$a^n \times a^m = a^{n+m}$$
2. Index law for dividing numbers of variables raised to a power is
$$a^n \div a^m = a^{n-m}$$
3. Index law for raising a variable written as a power to a power is
$$(a^n)^m = a^{n \times m}$$
4. When you expand a pair of brackets you multiply every term in the second bracket by every term in the first bracket.

Worked examples

a Work out

i $3x^4 \times 5x^6$ ii $\dfrac{12y^7}{4y^3}$ iii $(2f^3)^5$ iv $\dfrac{6a^6b^4 \times 4a^2b^5}{12a^5b^6}$

Answers

Deal with the whole numbers in front of the variables first.

$3 \times 5 = 15$ $12 \div 4 = 3$ $2^5 = 32$ $6 \times 4 \div 12 = 2$

Now deal with the powers or indices.

1. $15x^{4+6}$ 2. $3y^{7-3}$ 3. $32f^{3\times5}$ 1.2. $2a^{6+2-5}b^{4+5-6}$
   $= 15x^{10}$ $= 3y^4$ $= 32f^{15}$ $= 2a^3b^3$

b Expand and simplify

$(x - 4)(x + 6)$

Answer

4. $(x - 4) \quad (x + 6)$

$x \times x = x^2; x \times +6 = 6x$

$-4 \times x = -4x; -4 \times +6 = -24$ **OR**

$x^2 + 6x - 4x - 24$

$x^2 + 2x - 24$

$\times$	x	$+6$
x	x^2	$+6x$
-4	$-4x$	-24

$x^2 + 6x - 4x - 24$

$x^2 + 2x - 24$

Look out for

Any number or variable with a power or index of 0 is always 1, e.g. $a^0 = 1$; $25^0 = 1$

Key terms

Power

Index

Variable

Bracket

Expand

Simplify

Exam-style questions

1 Work out

a $\dfrac{12(y^3)^7}{16y^{15}}$ **[2]**

b $\dfrac{3a^5b^3 \times 5a^4b^5}{12(ab)^6}$ **[2]**

2 This shape is made from a large rectangle and a blue square.

Explain why the area of the red shape is $a^2 + 11a + 15$ **[3]**

Exam tip

Remember that powers and indices are the same.

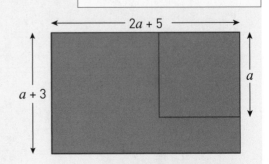

Using complex formulae and changing the subject of a formula

Rules

1. You can replace the variables or letters in a formula with positive and negative numbers.
2. Use BIDMAS and rules for dealing with adding, subtracting, multiplying and dividing positive and negative numbers to find the value of the missing letter.
3. Use inverses to change the subject of a formula so that the required variable or letter is on its own on one side of the formula or equation.

Worked examples

a Work out the value of p when $a = 2.5$, $b = -2$ and $c = -5$

$$p = \frac{2(a^2 - b^2)}{5 - 3c}$$

Answer

Firstly replace the variables or letters with their values.

$p = \frac{2((2.5)^2 - (-2)^2)}{5 - 3 \times (-5)}$ **①**

Then use BIDMAS and the positive and negative sign rules to get:

$p = \frac{2 \times 6.25 - 2 \times (+4)}{5 + 15}$ $(2.5^2 = 6.25, (-2)^2 = +4$ and $-3 \times -5 = +15)$ **②**

Then work it all out

$p = \frac{12.5 - 4}{20} = 8.5 \div 20 = 0.425$ **②**

b Make l the subject of the formula: $T = 2\pi\sqrt{\frac{l}{g}}$

Answer

You have to make the formula start with $l =$

so **first**, square both sides of the formula to get $T^2 = 4\pi^2 \frac{l}{g}$ **③**

Then multiply both sides by g to get: $gT^2 = 4\pi^2 l$ **③**

Last divide both sides by $4\pi^2$ to get: $\frac{gT^2}{4\pi^2} = l$ or $l = \frac{gT^2}{4\pi^2}$ **③**

Look out for

Like signs that multiplied or divided can be replaced with a **+** sign.

Unlike signs that multiplied or divided can be replaced with a **−** sign.

Whatever you **do to one side** of a formula you **must do to the other side** as well.

Key terms

Variable

Substitute

Formula

Equation

Exam-style questions

1 Work out the value of S when $u = -5$, $t = 10$ and $a = -4.9$
  $S = ut + at^2$ **[2]**

2 Make t the subject of this formula.
  $y = 5at^2 + 3s$ **[3]**

Exam tip

Remember to show the numbers when you substitute them into the formula.

CHECKED ANSWERS ☐

Identities

HIGH

Rules

❶ A formula is an equation for working out the value of the subject of the formula.

❷ An expression is a collection of terms or variables that occur in formulae, equations and identities.

❸ An equation can be solved to find the value of an unknown variable.

❹ An identity is always **true** for all possible values of the variables.

Worked examples

a Here is a list of collections of terms.
  i $5(2x - 3) = 10x - 15$
  ii $5(2x - 3) = 8x + 2$
  iii $12x^2y^3$
  iv $p = 5(2x - 3)$

Write down the special mathematical name for each collection.

Answers
  i This is an identity because both the expression on both sides of the equals sign is identical ❹

  ii This is an equation because the value of the variable has a unique value. The equation becomes $2x = 17$ or $x = 8.5$ ❸

  iii This is an expression; x and y are variables and 12 is the coefficient of the expression ❷

  iv This is a formula where p is the subject of the formula ❶

b Prove that the sum of two consecutive odd numbers is always a multiple of 4.

Answer
Firstly one needs to define our consecutive odd numbers as $2n + 1$ and then $2n + 3$.

Add the two expressions to get: $(2n + 1) + (2n + 3) = 4n + 4$

Factorise the expression by taking the 4 outside the bracket: $= 4(n + 1)$

Therefore since $4(n + 1)$ means $4 \times (n + 1)$, it is always a multiple of 4.

Look out for

If n is used to represent whole numbers then $2n$ is used to represent even numbers or multiples of 2 and $2n - 1$ or $2n + 1$ will then represent odd numbers.

Key terms

Variable

Term

Subject

Formula

Expression

Equation

Identity

Coefficient

Exam-style questions

1 Find the value of p and q to make this expression into an identity.
 $x^2 - 7x + 12 = (x + p)(x + q)$ **[2]**

2 Prove that the product of two odd numbers is always odd. **[4]**

Exam tip

Remember to always show each step in your working.

CHECKED ANSWERS

Linear sequences

Rules

❶ The difference is found by subtracting consecutive terms.
❷ If the difference between each term is always the same (common difference) then the sequence can always be written as $an + b$, this is the nth term.
❸ The value of a is always the common difference.
❹ Use the first term to find the value of b.
❺ To check if a number is in a sequence then make an equation with the nth term.
❻ By putting whole numbers (1, 2, 3…) into the nth term you can build up the sequence.

Worked examples

a Here is a number pattern: 4   10   16   22 …
  i Find the next term in the pattern.
  ii Find the nth term in the pattern.
  iii Explain why 102 is not a member of the pattern.

Look out for

Always check the difference between consecutive terms.

Answers
  i Common difference is 6 so next term is $22 + 6 = 28$ ❶
  ii nth term will be $6n + b$ ❷ ❸
    First term is 4 so $(6 \times 1) + b = 4$ so $b = 4 - 6 = -2$ ❹
    nth term is therefore $6n - 2$
  iii If 102 is in the sequence then $6n - 2 = 102$ ❺
    Add 2 to each side gives $6n = 104$
    Divide each side by 6 gives $n = 17\frac{1}{3}$
    For 102 to be in the series then the value of n must be a whole number because n is the term number.
    Therefore, 102 is not in the sequence.

Key terms

Term
Number sequence
Number pattern
Number series
Difference
Common difference
nth term

b The nth terms of two linear sequences are: $5n + 2$ and $30 - 6n$
  Explain if these two sequences have any terms that are common.

Answer
List the terms in the sequences ❻:

$5n + 2$ gives	7	12	17	22	27	32
$30 - 6n$ gives	24	18	12	6	0	-6

12 is in both sequences.

Exam-style questions

1 Here are some terms in a linear sequence.   7, …, 15, …, …, t

  a Find the value of term t. **[1]**
  b Find the nth term in the sequence **[2]**
  c Explain if 163 in the sequence. **[2]**

Exam hints

Always check your answer by listing the terms of the sequence.

2 For what value of n does the nth term of this linear sequence first become negative?

    55   51   47   43 …

You must show all your working. **[3]**

CHECKED ANSWERS

Special sequences

Rules

1. The difference between each term in a triangle number sequence goes up by one extra each time: 1, 3, 6, 10, 15, 21,...
2. The difference between each term in a square number sequence goes up by the same extra number each time: 1, 4, 9, 16, 25, 36, ...
3. The difference between each term in the Fibonacci sequence is also the Fibonacci sequence: 1, 1, 2, 3, 5, 8, 13, 21 ...
4. By putting whole numbers (1, 2, 3, ...) into the nth term you can build up each term in the sequence.

Worked examples

a Write down the first five terms of the sequences with nth terms
   i $n(n + 1)$
   ii $3n^2 + 1$

Answers
Put the values 1, 2, 3, 4, 5 instead of n to calculate the first 5 terms. ❹
   i $1 \times 2, 2 \times 3, 3 \times 4, 4 \times 5, 5 \times 6$ gives 2, 6, 12, 20, 30
   ii $3 \times 1^2 + 1, 3 \times 2^2 + 1, 3 \times 3^2 + 1, 3 \times 4^2 + 1, 3 \times 5^2 + 1$, gives
       $3 \times 1 + 1, 3 \times 4 + 1, 3 \times 9 + 1, 3 \times 16 + 1, 3 \times 25 + 1$,
       or 4, 13, 28, 49, 76

b Find the nth terms of these number patterns.
   i   2, 5, 10, 17, 26, ...
   ii 4, 12, 24, 40, 60, ...

Answers
   i   The difference between each term is 3, 5, 7, 9; the difference goes up in two's so it must be a square number pattern. ❷
       The nth term is $n^2 + 1$, one more than the square numbers.
   ii The difference between each term is 8, 12, 16, 20; the difference goes up in 4 extra each time so it much be a triangular number pattern. ❶
       The nth term is $2n(n + 1)$, four times the triangle numbers.

Look out for

The nth term for square number is n^2.

The nth term for triangle number is $\frac{n(n+1)}{2}$.

Key terms

Sequence

Triangle numbers

Square numbers

Fibonacci numbers

Term

nth term

Difference

Exam-style questions

1 Rachel makes a pattern from squares.

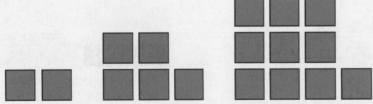

   a   Find the nth term of Rachel's pattern. **[2]**
   b   How many squares are there in pattern number 20? **[1]**

2 Here is a number pattern   6, 12, 20, 30, 42, ...

   Find the nth term of the pattern. **[3]**

Exam tip

Always look for the difference between each term in a number pattern to help decide which type of pattern it is.

CHECKED ANSWERS

Quadratic sequences

Rules

① In a quadratic sequence the difference between the terms increases by the same number each time.

② In a quadratic sequence the difference between the differences is always the same number. This is called the second difference.

Sequence		2		8		18		32		50		72
First difference			6		10		14		18		22		
Second difference				4		4		4		4			

③ By putting whole numbers (1, 2, 3, ...) into the nth term you can build up the sequence.

Worked examples

a The nth term of a quadratic sequence is: $2n^2 - 1$. The mth term of a different quadratic sequence is: $98 - (m + 1)^2$. Which numbers are in both sequences?

Answer

List both sequences by putting in values of 1, 2, 3, etc. for n.

$2n^2 - 1$ gives: $\quad 2 \times 1^2 - 1, 2 \times 2^2 - 1, 2 \times 3^2 - 1$, etc. ③

$98 - (m + 1)^2$ gives: $\quad 98 - (1 + 1)^2, 98 - (2 + 1)^2, 98 - (3 + 1)^2$, etc. ③

Sequences are: 1, 7, 17, 31, 49, 71, 97, ...

and: 94, 89, 82, 73, 62, 49, 34, 17, −2, ...

So 17 and 49 are in both sequences.

b Find the nth term of this sequence: 3, 7, 13, 21, 31, 43, ...

Answer

Sequence		3		7		13		21		31		43
① First difference			4		6		8		10		12		
② Second difference				2		2		2		2			

As the second difference is always 2, the sequence is quadratic.

The sequence builds by $1 \times 2 + 1, 2 \times 3 + 1, 3 \times 4 + 1, 4 \times 5 + 1$, etc.

The nth term is: $n(n + 1) + 1$

Look out for

If the second difference is 2 then the coefficient of n^2 is always 1.

Watch for triangular numbers in a quadratic sequence.

Key terms

Quadratic

Sequence

Difference

Second difference

Exam-style questions

1 The nth term of a quadratic sequence is:
$(n + 1)^2 - 2$
The mth term of a different quadratic sequence is: $50 - m^2$
Which numbers are in both sequences? **[3]**

2 Find the nth term of this sequence:
7, 13, 29, 37, 55, ... **[3]**

Exam tips

Look out for square numbers in the sequences.

If the second difference is 2, start with n^2.

If the second difference is 4, start with $2n^2$.

If the second difference is 6, start with $3n^2$.

CHECKED ANSWERS

Geometric progressions

Rules

1. To get the next term in a geometric progression (or sequence) you always multiply the previous term by the same number.
2. The number you multiply each term by is called the common ratio.
3. To find the common ratio you divide the second term by the first and the third term by the second and so on.
4. You start with a number e.g. 5
   You multiply by the common ratio e.g. 3
   The sequence becomes 5, 5×3, $5 \times 3 \times 3$, $5 \times 3 \times 3 \times 3$ etc.
   5, 15, 45, 135, 405, ...

Worked examples

a Find the next term in these sequences.

| i | 3 | 12 | 48 | 192 | 768 |
| ii | 50 | 5 | 0.5 | 0.05 | 0.005 |

Answers

i   The common ratio is $12 \div 3 = 4$ check with $48 \div 12 = 4$ ❸
    The next term is $768 \times 4 = 3072$ ❹

ii The common ratio is $5 \div 50 = 0.1$ check with $0.5 \div 5 = 0.1$ ❸
    The next term is $0.005 \times 0.1 = 0.0005$ ❹

b Dave bought a van for £5000. Its value at the end of each year forms a geometric progression. The common ratio of the geometric progression is 0.9

i   Find the value after 2 years.

ii After how many years will the van be worth less than £3000?

Answers

i $5000 \times 0.9 \times 0.9 = £4050$ ❹

ii After 1 year it is $5000 \times 0.9 = £4500$ ❹
    After 2 years it is $4500 \times 0.9 = £4050$
    After 3 years it is $4050 \times 0.9 = £3645$
    After 4 years it is $3645 \times 0.9 = £3280.50$
    After 5 years it is $3280.5 \times 0.9 = £2952.45$
    The value drops below £3000 after 5 years.

Look out for

The connection between the terms is always found by multiplying each term by the common ratio.

Key terms

Common ratio

Term

Geometric progression

Sequence

Exam-style questions

1. The first term of a geometric progression is 12. The third term of the geometric progression is 75.

   a   Find the common ratio of the geometric progression. **[2]**
   b   Work out the 6th term of the progression. **[2]**

2. Jane invests £5000. The value of her investment at the end of each year forms a geometric progression. The common ratio of the geometric progression is 1.03.

   Find the value of her investment after 5 years. **[3]**

Exam tip

Work out the common ratio first and then work through the sequence term by term.

CHECKED ANSWERS

Mixed exam-style questions

1 Nigel uses this formula to change between degrees Fahrenheit and degrees Celsius.

$$C = \frac{5F - 160}{9}$$

The average normal temperature of a human body is 98.6 °F.
a What is 98.6 °F in degrees Celsius? [2]
b What temperature is the same in degrees Celsius as it is in degrees Fahrenheit? [3]

2 Bobbi uses this formula to work out the time, t minutes, it takes to cook a chicken of weight w kg.
$t = 40w + 20$
Bobbi wants a chicken weighing 2 kg to be cooked at 12 noon. At what time should she put the chicken into the oven? [3]

3 A square has a perimeter of $(40x + 60)$ cm. A regular pentagon has the same perimeter as the square.
Show that the difference between the length of the sides of the two shapes is $(2x + 3)$ cm. [3]

4 Mrs Jones organises a school trip to the theatre for 42 people.
She takes children and adults on the trip.
Each adult paid £40 for their ticket.
Each child paid £16 for their ticket.
The total cost of the tickets was £1080.
How many adults went on the trip? [4]

5 The red square is formed by cutting the 4 blue right-angled triangles, each with base of $x + 2$ and a height of $5x - 3$, from each corner as shown below.

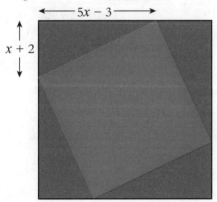

Show that the area of the red square is $13(2x^2 - 2x + 1)$ [5]

6 Here is a T shape drawn on part of a 10 by 10 grid. The shaded T is called T_2 because 2 is the smallest number in the T.
T_2 is the sum of all the numbers in the T shape; so $T_2 = 45$.
a Find an expression, in terms of n, for T_n [3]
b Explain why T_n cannot equal 130. [2]

1	2	3	4	5	6
11	12	13	14	15	16
21	22	23	24	25	26
31	32	33	34	35	36
41	42	43	44	45	46

7 Rhys has a beehive. There are 800 bees in the hive at the start of week 7. There are 1600 bees in the hive at the start of week 5. Assuming that the population of bees is decreasing as a GP.
a Show that there were 6400 bees at the start of week 1. [2]
b Estimate the number of bees in the hive at the start of week 10. [3]

Plotting graphs of linear functions

Rules

1. Always draw up a table of values to help plot the points on the grid.
2. Start with the value 0 and put in positive values first.
3. Plot the points and join with a straight line.
4. You can use the graph to read off values from one axis to the other.

Worked examples

a The time it takes to cook a chicken is given by the formula $T = 20w + 20$
  i Draw a table of values for $T = 20w + 20$
  ii Draw the graph of T for values of w from 0 to 5 pounds in weight (w).
  iii Use your graph to find the time (T) it takes to cook a $3\frac{1}{2}$ pound chicken.

Answers
i ❶ ❷

w	0	1	2	3	4	5
$20w$	0	20	40	60	80	100
20	20	20	20	20	20	20
$T = 20w + 20$	20	40	60	80	100	120

ii Draw graph. ❸

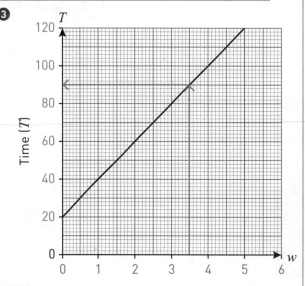

iii Draw a vertical line up from $3\frac{1}{2}$ on the w axis to the graph and then from the graph draw a horizontal line to the T axis. ❹
This gives an answer of 90 mins.

b Here is a table of values for $y = 2x + 1$.

x	−3	−2	−1	0	1	2	3
y							

i Copy and complete the table of values.
ii Draw the graph of $y = 2x + 1$.
iii Find the value of x when $y = 4$.

Look out for

Always work out the positive values first in a table of values.

Make sure the line is straight when you draw it.

Key terms

Variable

Table of values

Axis

Exam tip

Always show how you read off from the graph by drawing in the straight lines.

→

Answers

i   First work out the positive values of y. Then work out the negative values. (They should follow the same pattern.) ❶ ❷

x	–3	–2	–1	0	1	2	3
y	–5	–3	–1	1	3	5	7

ii   Graph drawn. ❸

iii $x = 1.5$ when $y = 4$ ❹

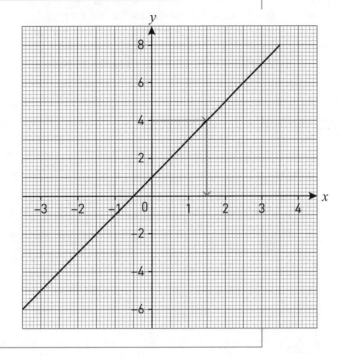

1   Liam hires a car. He pays £40 for the first day then £20 for each extra day.
   a   Draw the graph of the cost of hiring the car. **[2]**
   b   Liam has £150 to spend on car hire. For how many days can Liam hire the car? **[2]**

2   Here is a table of values for $y = 2x - 1$

x	–3	–2	–1	0	1	2	3
y							

   a   Copy and complete the table of values. **[2]**
   b   Draw the graph of $y = 2x - 1$. **[3]**
   c   Find the value of x when $y = 4$. **[2]**

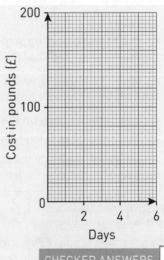

CHECKED ANSWERS

Real-life graphs

REVISED ☐

LOW

Rules

1. The maximum value is the highest point on the graph.
2. The minimum value is the lowest point on the graph.
3. The steeper the line on a graph means the greater the rate of change.
4. The less steep the line on a graph means the lower the rate of change.
5. If the line is horizontal the rate of change is zero.

Worked example

Here are four graphs.

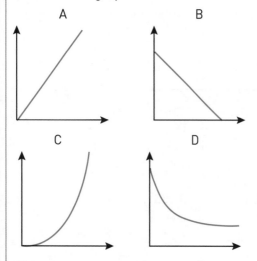

Write down a situation that each of the graphs could describe.

Answer

A As one variable goes up so does the other. These graphs can be used for conversion graphs and where the more you buy the more you pay.

B As one variable goes up the other variable goes down. It can show the fuel left in a car's fuel tank as it goes on a journey.

C As one variable goes up the other variable goes up faster. It can show an increase in population e.g. rabbits. ③

D As one variable goes up the other variable goes down but less slowly as it goes down. It can show the temperature of a cup of tea when left to cool. ④

Look out for

Distance time graphs and conversion graphs.

Key terms

Variable

Axes

Relationship

Maximum

Minimum

Rate of change

Gradient

Exam tip

Use sentences in worded answers.

Exam-style questions

Here is a travel graph of Jo's trip to the shops and back. She had to stop at some roadworks on her way to the shops.
a What time did Jo leave home? **[1]**
b How much time did Jo have to spend at the roadworks? **[1]**
c How much time did she spend at the shops? **[1]**
d At what time did Jo get home again? **[1]**
e How far is Jo's home from the shops? **[1]**
f How much time did it take Jo to get to the shops? **[1]**
g How much time did it take Jo to get home from the shops? **[1]**
h Work out Jo's average speed from the shops to home. **[2]**

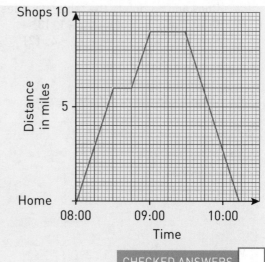

CHECKED ANSWERS ☐

The equation of a straight line

Rules

1. Vertical lines which are parallel to the y-axis have the equation $x = $ a number.
2. Horizontal lines which are parallel to the x-axis have the equation $y = $ a number.
3. Slanting lines have the equation $y = mx + c$
4. To find m, the gradient of a slanting line, find the coordinates of two points on the line and divide the difference of their y-coordinates by the difference of their x-coordinates.
5. The value of c is the y-coordinate of the point where the line crosses the y-axis.

Look out for

Draw a diagram to help answer the question.

Parallel lines have the same gradient.

Lines with a positive gradient go from bottom left to top right.

Lines with a negative gradient go from top left to bottom right.

Worked example

a Here is a straight line drawn on a coordinate grid. Find the equation of the line.

Answer

Two points on the line are $(-1, 2)$ and $(1, 6)$ ③

The gradient of the line is found by finding the lengths of the horizontal and vertical lines and dividing them.

The vertical length is $6 - 2 = 4$ units and the horizontal length $1 - -1 = 2$ units

Divide the vertical length by the horizontal length.

The gradient is $4 \div 2 = 2$ ④

The intercept, c, on the y-axis is at 4 ⑤

The gradient is positive as it goes from bottom left to top right.

Therefore the equation of the line is $y = 2x + 4$.

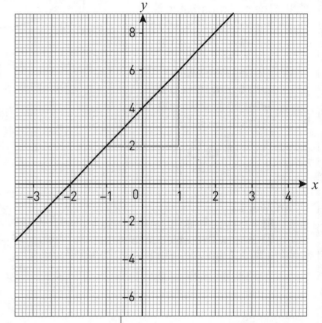

b Here are some straight lines. Which of them are parallel?

P $y = 3x + 2$ **Q** $y + 3x = 2$
R $3y = 3 - 9x$ **S** $9x + 3y = 12$
T $3x - y = 5$

Answer

Firstly write all the equations in the form $y = mx + c$

P $y = 3x + 2$ **Q** $y = -3x + 2$
R $y = -3x + 1$ **S** $y = -3x + 4$ **T** $y = 3x - 5$

Now check for the ones that have the same gradient. **P** and **T** have the same gradient (3) and also **Q**, **R** and **S** have the same (−3).

Key terms

Gradient

Intercept

Parallel

Exam-style questions

1. Write down an equation of a line that is parallel to $y = 2x + 3$ that passes through the point $(0, -1)$ **[2]**
2. Here are some straight lines.
   P $y = 2x + 3$ **Q** $y + 2x = 1$
   R $2y = 3 - 4x$ **S** $8x - 4y = 12$ **T** $6x - 3y = 15$
   Which of them are parallel? **[3]**

Exam tip

Always write your equations in the form $y = mx + c$

CHECKED ANSWERS

Plotting quadratic and cubic graphs

Rules

1. Always draw a table of values to help plot the points on the grid.
2. Start with the value 0 and put in positive values first.
3. Plot the points and join them with a smooth curved line.
4. You can use the graph to read off values from one axis to the other.
5. A quadratic graph will be in the shape of a letter U or an ∩.
6. A cubic graph will be in the shape of a letter ∽.

Worked example

a   Here is the graph of
$y = x^2 - 3x - 2$ for values of x
from −2 to +4. ❸ ❹ ❺
   i   What is the minimum
value of $x^2 - 3x - 2$?
   ii For what values of x
is y negative?

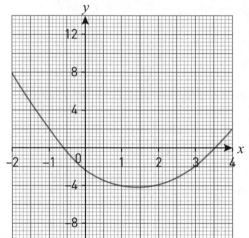

Answers
   i   The minimum value is at
the bottom of the U. The
minimum value is when
x is 1.5 so $y = -4.25$
   ii y is negative when it
goes below the x-axis so
between $x = -0.6$ and 3.6

b   i   Draw the graph of $y = x^3 - 5x + 2$
for values of x from
$-3 + 3$ ❸ ❹ ❻
   ii Solve the equation
$x^3 - 5x + 2 = 0$

Answers
   i   ❶ First you make a table of values.
   ❷ Start with 0 which means that
$y = +2$. Then work out the positive
values of x first.

   Finally do the negative values.

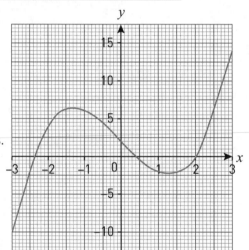

x	−3	−2	−1	0	1	2	3
x^3	−27	−8	−1	0	1	8	27
$-5x$	15	10	5	0	−5	−10	−15
$+2$	2	2	2	2	2	2	2
$y =$	−10	4	6	2	−2	0	14

   ii The solutions to the equation are where the curve cuts the x-axis at $x = -2.4$ or at $x = 0.4$ or at $x = 2$

Exam-style questions

1 a   Draw the graph of $y = x^2 - 4x + 3$ for values of x from −2 to + 4 **[4]**
   b   Use your graph to solve the equation $x^2 - 4x + 3 = 0$ **[2]**
2 Draw the graph of $y = x^3 - 5x + 2$ for values of x from −3 to +3 **[4]**

Exam tip

Always look for solving an
equation as the last part to a
graph question.

Finding equations of straight lines

Rules

1. Slanting lines have the equation $y = mx + c$
2. m is the gradient of the line and measures how steep the line is.
3. To find m, the gradient of a slanting line, find the coordinates of two points on the line and divide the difference of their y-coordinates by the difference of their x-coordinates.
4. The value of c, the intercept on the y-axis, is the y-coordinate of the point where the line crosses the y-axis.

Worked examples

a **L** and **M** are two straight lines. **L** has a gradient of 3 and crosses the y-axis at $(0, 4)$. **M** has a gradient of -2 and passes through the point $(-1, 5)$. Find the equations of the two lines.

Answer

The equation of **L** is $y = 3x + 4$. ❶

3 is the gradient of the line so is the value of m. ❷

$(0, 4)$ is on the y-axis so the value of c is 4 ❹

The equation of **M** is $y = -2x + c$ ❶

-2 is the gradient of the line so the value of m is -2 ❷

As we do not know the value of c you need to put the coordinates $(-1, 5)$ into the equation so with $x = -1$ and $y = 5$ you get $5 = -2 \times -1 + c$ or $5 = +2 + c$ so $c = 3$ ❹

The equation of **M** is $y = -2x + 3$

b **P** and **Q** are two straight lines. **P** is parallel to the line $2x + y = 5$ and passes through $(2, 9)$. **Q** passes through the points $(-2, 7)$ and $(4, -5)$. Find the equations of the two lines.

Answer

P is parallel to $2x + y = 5$. This can be written as $y = -2x + 5$ so -2 is the gradient of the line so the value of m is -2 ❷. The equation of **P** is therefore $y = -2x + c$ ❶. To find the value of c use a coordinate that lies on the line, $(2, 9)$, put this into the equation so with $x = 2$ and $y = 9$ you get $9 = -2 \times 2 + c$ or $9 = -4 + c$ so $c = 13$ ❹.

The equation of **P** is $y = -2x + 13$. Always sketch the line so you can check the gradient.

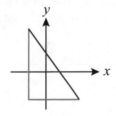

Gradient is $(7 - -5) \div (-2 - 4) = 12 \div -6 = -2$ ❸

The equation of **Q** is $y = -2x + c$ ❶

Substitute a point into the equation e.g. $7 = -2 \times -2 + c$ so $c = 7 - 4 = 3$ ❹

The equation of **Q** is $y = -2x + 3$

Look out for

Parallel lines have the same gradient.

Lines with a positive gradient go from bottom left to top right.

Lines with a negative gradient go from top left to bottom right.

Key terms

Gradient

Intercept

Equation

Parallel

Exam tip

If given the coordinates, always sketch a diagram so you can check whether the gradient of the line is positive or negative.

Exam-style questions

1 Find the equation of the straight line that is parallel to $y = 3x + 2$ and passes through $(1, 6)$ **[3]**

2 Find the equation of the straight line that passes through the points $(-2, 5)$ and $(3, -5)$ **[3]**

CHECKED ANSWERS

Quadratic functions

Rules

❶ A quadratic function always has an equation $y = ax^2 + bx + c$ where $a \neq 0$.

❷ When a is positive the graph will be U-shaped and have a minimum value.

❸ When a is negative the graph will be ∩-shaped and have a maximum value.

❹ The graph of a quadratic function is always symmetrical and the line of symmetry is parallel to the y-axis and passes through the maximum or minimum.

❺ The roots of the quadratic equation $ax^2 + bx + c = 0$ are the solutions to the equation and the values of x where the curve cuts the x-axis.

Worked example

Here is the graph of a quadratic function.

i Write down the roots when the function = 0

ii Write down the equation of the line of symmetry of the function.

iii Write down the value of x for which the function has a minimum value.

iv Find the equation of the function.

Look out for

The turning point of a quadratic can either be a maximum or a minimum.

Key terms

Quadratic

Intercepts

Roots

Turning point

Maximum

Minimum

Answers

i The roots of the equation are the values of x where the curve cuts the x-axis. These are –1 and 3 ❺

ii The line of symmetry is $x = 1$ ❹

iii The minimum value of the function is –4. This occurs at (1, –4) so the value of x is 1 ❹

iv As the roots are –1 and +3 then the solution of the quadratic equation is $x = -1$ or $x = 3$, so $x + 1 = 0$ or $x - 3 = 0$

You now need to combine these together into an equation. This means $(x + 1)(x - 3) = 0$. So an equation is $x^2 - 3x + x - 3 = 0$ or $x^2 - 2x - 3 = 0$ ❷

The function is therefore $y = x^2 - 2x - 3$ ❶

Exam tip

It is always a good idea to draw a sketch of the graph if you are not given one in the question.

Exam-style questions

1 A quadratic equation has roots –2 and +4 and passes through the point (0, –8). Sketch the graph and write the function in the form $y = ax^2 + bx + c$ **[5]**

2 a Sketch the graph of $y = 9 - x^2$ **[3]**

  b Find the roots of the equation $9 - x^2 = 0$ **[1]**

  c Write down the coordinates of the maximum point of the graph. **[1]**

CHECKED ANSWERS

Polynomial and reciprocal functions

Rules

1. Straight line graphs are in the form $y = mx + c$
2. Quadratic graphs are in the form $y = ax^2 + bx + c$ and are in the shapes of a U or ∩.
3. Cubic graphs are in the form $y = ax^3 + bx^2 + cx + d$ and are in the shape of an ∽ or ∾.
4. Reciprocal graphs are in the form $y = \frac{k}{x}$ and have two parts.

   They approach but never touch two straight lines; the straight lines are are called asymptotes.

Worked example

Here is the graph of $y = 6 - x^2$

i   On the same grid, draw the graph of $y = \frac{1}{2x}$

ii Write down the equations of the asymptotes.

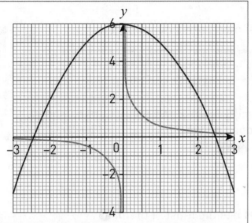

Answers

i   First work out a table of values. ④

x	−3	−2	−1	0	1	2	3
$y = \frac{1}{2x}$	−0.17	−0.25	−0.5	No value	0.5	0.25	0.17

As there is no value for $\frac{1}{2x}$ when $x = 0$ you will need to use values of x between
$-1 \leqslant x < 0$ and $0 < x \leqslant 1$

x	−0.5	−0.2	−0.1	0	0.1	0.2	0.5
$y = \frac{1}{2x}$	−1	−2.5	−5	No value	5	2.5	1

ii The asymptotes are $y = 0$ (the x-axis) and $x = 0$ (the y-axis). ④

Look out for

When you have reciprocal graphs there will always be one value that you cannot calculate, normally when $x = 0$

Key terms

Plot

Sketch

Straight line

Quadratic

Cubic

Reciprocal

Asymptote

Exam-style questions

1 a   On the same grid sketch the graphs of $y = x$, $y = x^2$ and $y = x^3$ **[3]**
  b   Which points lie on all three lines? **[2]**

2 Jill's car fuel consumption, f, changes as her speed, s, increases.

  The fuel consumption is given by the formula $f = 60 - \frac{60}{s}$

  What value is the fuel consumption approaching as she increases her speed?

  You must explain your answer. **[4]**

Exam tips

Draw or plot means a graph needs to be accurate.

Sketch means you need show the main features of the graph.

CHECKED ANSWERS ☐

Linear inequalities

Rules

1. When you solve an inequality you need to keep the sign pointing the same way.
2. Changing the direction of the inequality sign is the same as multiplying by –1 so if you swap sides in an inequality you swap signs. So if $-5 > x$ then $-x > 5$ so $x < -5$.
3. Use the same techniques to solve an inequality as you do to solve an equation.
4. A filled-in circle on a number line means the inequality is $\geqslant$ or $\leqslant$. ●
5. An open circle on a number line means the inequality is $<$ or $>$. ○
6. Always define your variables when you solve an inequality problem.

Worked examples

a **i** Write down the inequality shown on this number line.

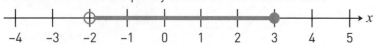

Answer

The left hand end of the inequality is at –2 and the right hand end is at 3. ❹ ❺ The circle at –2 is open and the circle at 3 is filled in so the inequality is: $-2 < x \leqslant 3$. ❹ ❺

ii Solve the inequality $5x + 3 > 7x - 4$

Answer

Keep the xs on the side that has the most of them. ❶

So $-5x$ from each side: $3 > 2x - 4$ ❸

Now add 4 to each side: $7 > 2x$

Divide by 2 gives: $3.5 > x$

Swap sides and change sign: $x < 3.5$ ❷

b Amy is 3 years older than Beth. Ceri is twice as old as Beth. The total of their ages is less than 39.
Show that Ami must be less than 12 years old.

Answer

First define your variable so let Ami's age be x ❻. Then write down the other ages.

Beth will be 3 years less than Ami: $x - 3$

Ceri's age will be twice Beth's age: $2(x - 3)$

Then set up the inequality: $x + x - 3 + 2(x - 3) < 39$

Then solve it: $2x - 3 + 2x - 6 < 39$ ❸. $4x - 9 < 39$

so $4x < 48$ so $x < 12$ and therefore Ami is less than 12 years old.

Look out for

Always use the same techniques for solving inequalities as you do to solve equations.

Key terms

$<$ less than

$>$ greater than

$\leqslant$ less than or equal to

$\geqslant$ greater than or equal to

Exam-style questions

1 **a** On a number line write down the inequality $-3 \leqslant x < 4$ **[2]**
   b Solve the inequality $3(2y - 4) \leqslant 6$ **[3]**

2 Bobbi thinks of a whole number, she adds 10 to it and then divides by 5. The answer is less than 4.
What numbers could Bobbi have thought of? **[4]**

Exam tip

Always check the answer to inequalities by substituting your answer back into the question.

CHECKED ANSWERS

Solving simultaneous equations by elimination and substitution

Rules

❶ If the coefficients of both of the variables are different then you must multiply the equations by a number so that the coefficients of one variable are the same.

❷ To eliminate the variable if the coefficients have the same sign you subtract the two equations; if the signs are different then you add the two equations.

❸ Once you have found the value of the other variable you substitute it into one of the original equations to find the eliminated variable.

❹ If the coefficient of one of the variables is 1 then rearrange that equation so that it becomes the subject e.g. $x =$ or $y =$

❺ Substitute the rearranged equation into the second equation.

❻ Solve the new equation for one variable.

❼ Substitute this variable into the first equation to find the other variable.

Worked examples

a Solve $3x + 4y = 2$ eqn. 1
$4x - 5y = 13$ eqn. 2

Answer

The coefficients of the variables x and y are not the same so you need to multiply each equation by a number to make them the same.

You could multiply eqn. 1 by 4 and eqn. 2 by 3 so that the x coeff. is 12

You could multiply eqn. 1 by 5 and eqn. 2 by 4 so that the y coeff. is 20

It is easier to add than subtract so we eliminate the y

$3x + 4y = 2$ eqn. 1 × 5 gives $15x + 20y = 10$ ❶
$4x - 5y = 13$ eqn. 2 × 4 gives $16x - 20y = 52 +$ ❶

Adding the two equations gives $\overline{31x \qquad = 62}$ so $x = 2$ ❷

Substituting $x = 2$ into eqn. 1 gives ❸

    $3 \times 2 + 4y = 2$, so $6 + 4y = 2$; this means $4y = -4$ so $y = -1$

b Solve $2x + y = 3$ eqn. 1
$3x - 4y = 10$ eqn. 2

Answer

The coefficient of y in eqn. 1 is equal to 1 so we rearrange eqn. 1 to be $y = 3 - 2x$ ❹

We substitute $y = 3 - 2x$ into eqn. 2 to get $3x - 4(3 - 2x) = 10$ ❺

Multiply out the bracket to get $3x - 12 + 8x = 10$ ❻

Simplify the left-hand side to get $11x - 12 = 10$ ❻

So $11x = 22$ so $x = 2$ ❻

Substituting $x = 2$ into $y = 3 - 2x$ gives
                $y = 3 - 2 \times 2$, so $y = 3 - 4$; this means $y = -1$

Look out for

The coefficients of the variables need to be made the same for the elimination method.

If one of the variables has a coefficient of 1 use the substitution method.

Key terms

Simultaneous equations

Coefficient

Variable

Subject

Substitute

Eliminate

Solve

Exam tip

Always check your answer by substituting back into the original equations.

Exam-style questions

1 Solve $2a + 3b = 13$
     $5a - 2b = 4$ **[3]**

2 A coach company has s superior coaches and d ordinary coaches. The company has four times as many ordinary coaches as superior coaches. An ordinary coach has 50 seats and a superior coach has 25 seats. The coach company has a total of 675 seats available. How many coaches of each type does the company have? **[4]**

CHECKED ANSWERS ☐

Using graphs to solve simultaneous equations

Rules

❶ Form an equation for each part of your problem in the form $y = mx + c$
❷ On a coordinate grid draw the two lines so that they intersect.
❸ The solution of the simultaneous equations are the coordinates of the point of intersection.

Worked examples

a G-gas and P-gas sell gas. Green gas charges £10 a month and 20p a unit. Power-gas charges £20 a month and 10p a unit. Which company is cheaper?

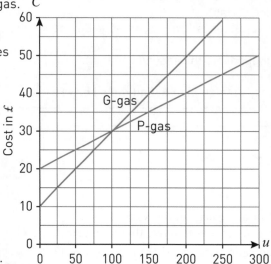

Answer
Firstly set up equations.

$C = 0.2u + 10$ for G-gas. ❶

$C = 0.1u + 20$ for P-gas. ❶

Use the same units (£).

Then draw the graphs. ❷

Use the intercept and gradient to get the line.

The lines cross at (100, 30) ❸. 100 units of gas are used and the cost is £30.

This means that G-gas is cheaper up to 100 units.
At 100 units both companies charge the same amount.
After 100 units P-gas is cheaper.

b Here is the graph of the circle $x^2 + y^2 = 9$

Find the solution to the following simultaneous equations.

$x^2 + y^2 = 9$ and

$y + 2x = 2$

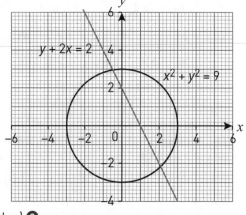

Answer
The solution is where the two lines cross so you need to draw in the straight line $y = -2x + 2$ on the grid.

Intersect at $x = -0.5$, $y = 3.0$ and $x = 2.1$ $y = -2.2$ (correct to 1 d.p.) ❸

Look out for

When you set up an equation you need to make sure that you use the same units throughout the equations.

Where the lines cross is the solution to the simultaneous equations.

Key terms

Simultaneous equations

Gradient and intercept of straight line graphs

Intersection of two lines

Exam-style questions

1 Use a graphical method to find the point where the lines $x + 3y = 2$ and $y = 3x + 4$ cross. **[4]**

2 Here are the tariffs for two mobile phone companies. **M-mobile** charges £20 a month and data costs 50p per Mbyte. **Peach** charges £10 a month and data costs 75p per Mbyte. Explain which company is cheaper. **[5]**

Exam tip

Be careful when you read off the results of the point of intersection of the lines when the scales are different on the two axes.

Factorising quadratics of the form $x^2 + bx + c$

Rules

1. A quadratic expression of the form $x^2 + bx + c$ can sometimes be factorised into two brackets.
2. When the coefficient of x^2 is 1 then each bracket will start with x e.g. $(x \quad)(x \quad)$
3. The number terms in the brackets multiply to give the number term c in the quadratic expression.
4. The number terms in the brackets add to give the coefficient of x in the quadratic expression.

Worked examples

a Factorise $x^2 + 5x + 6$

Answer

The number term is + 6 so the numbers in the brackets multiply to give + 6 which means they could be +1 and +6 **or** –1 and –6 **or** +2 and +3 **or** –2 and –3.

The coefficient of x is 5 so the two numbers need to add up to 5 which means they will need to be 2 and 3.

So $x^2 + 5x + 6 = (x + 2)(x + 3)$ because $x^2 + (2 + 3)x + 2 \times 3$.

b Factorise $x^2 - 5x + 6$

Answer

The number term is + 6 so the numbers in the brackets multiply to + 6 which means they could be +1 and +6 **or** –1 and –6 **or** +2 and +3 **or** –2 and –3.

The coefficient of x is –5 so the two numbers need to add up to –5 which means they will need to be –2 and –3.

So $x^2 - 5x + 6 = (x - 2)(x - 3)$ because $x^2 + (-2 + -3)x + -2 \times -3$.

c Factorise $x^2 - x - 6$

Answer

The number term is –6 so the numbers in the brackets multiply to –6 which means they could be +1 and –6 **or** –1 and +6 **or** +2 and –3 **or** –2 and +3

The coefficient of x is –1 so the two numbers need to add up to –1 which means they will need to be +2 and –3

So $x^2 - x - 6 = (x + 2)(x - 3)$ because $x^2 + (+2 + -3)x + +2 \times -3$.

d Factorise $x^2 + x - 6$

Answer

The number term is –6 so the numbers in the brackets multiply to –6 which means they could be +1 and –6 **or** –1 and +6 **or** +2 and –3 **or** –2 and +3.

The coefficient of x is +1 so the two numbers need to add up to +1 which means they will need to be –2 and +3.

So $x^2 + x - 6 = (x - 2)(x + 3)$ because $x^2 + (-2 + 3)x + -2 \times +3$.

e Factorise $x^2 - 25$. This is called the **difference of two squares**.

Answer

You get $x^2 - 25 = (x + 5)(x - 5)$ because $x^2 + (+5 + -5)x + +5 \times -5$.

Key terms

Quadratic expression

Factorise

Coefficient

Brackets

Look out for

When you have to factorise the difference of two squares $x^2 - y^2$ you get $(x + y)$ and $(x - y)$ so $x^2 - y^2 = (x + y)(x - y)$.

Exam-style questions

1 Factorise $x^2 + 6x + 8$ **[2]**
2 Factorise $x^2 - 2x - 8$ **[2]**
3 Factorise $x^2 + 2x - 8$ **[2]**
4 Factorise $x^2 - 6x + 8$ **[2]**
5 Factorise $x^2 - 16$ **[2]**

CHECKED ANSWERS

Exam tip

After you have factorised a quadratic expression, always multiply out the brackets to make sure you get back to the original expression.

Solve equations by factorising

Rules

❶ A quadratic equation has a term in x^2 and to solve it, it must always equal 0
❷ Factorise the quadratic function that equals 0
❸ Make two equations from the factorised expressions; both equal to 0
❹ Solve the two equations to get your solutions.

Worked examples

a Solve $x^2 - 5x = 0$

Answer

Quadratic equation = 0 so you can factorise it into $x(x - 5) = 0$ ❶ ❷

So you need to make two equations, either $x = 0$ or $x - 5 = 0$ ❸

This means that either $x = 0$ or $x = 5$ ❹

b Solve $x^2 + 3x - 10 = 0$

Answer

Quadratic equation = 0 so you can factorise it into $(x - 2)(x + 5) = 0$ ❶ ❷

So you need to make two equations, either $x - 2 = 0$ or $x + 5 = 0$ ❸

This means that either $x = 2$ or $x = -5$ ❹

c Solve $x^2 - 5x = 14$

Answer

This quadratic equation does not equal 0 so you need to re-arrange it into $x^2 - 5x - 14 = 0$ ❶, which can now be factorised into $(x + 2)(x - 7) = 0$ ❷

Now you need to make two equations either $x + 2 = 0$ or $x - 7 = 0$ ❸

This means that either $x = -2$ or $x = 7$ ❹

d A rectangle's length is 5 cm longer than its width. The area of the rectangle is 24 cm². Find the length and width of the rectangle.

Answer

Let the width be x cm. The length will be $(x + 5)$ cm.

Since the area is 24 cm², the equation $x(x + 5) = 24$ can be formed. This needs to be rearranged by multiplying out the bracket into $x^2 + 5x = 24$. Now you need to make the equation = 0 so that $x^2 + 5x - 24 = 0$

Now you factorise to get $(x - 3)(x + 8) = 0$

This means $x = 3$ cm or $x = -8$ cm.

As you cannot have a negative length for a measurement, $x = 3$ cm and the answers are length is 8 cm; width is 3 cm.

$(x + 5)$ cm

x cm | Area = 24 cm²

Look out for

Make sure that the quadratic equation always equals zero. If it does not, then rearrange the equation.

When you have an equation in x^2 then there will be two solutions.

Key terms

Quadratic equation

Solve

Factorise

Exam-style questions

1 Solve
  a $x^2 + 4x - 12 = 0$ **[3]**
  b $x^2 - 5x = 0$ **[3]**
  c $x^2 - 7x = 18$ **[3]**
  d $x^2 - 25 = 0$ **[3]**

2 Ben thinks of a number. He adds 5 to the number and squares his answer. His final answer is 49. What numbers could Ben have been thinking about? **[4]**

CHECKED ANSWERS

Exam tips

You might have to form the equation in order to solve a problem.

Make sure your values for x make sense.

Mixed exam-style questions

1 Sid hires a car from **Cars 4 U**.
   a Find the cost of hiring a car for 4 days
   from **Cars 4 U**.
   b The cost of hiring a car from **Cars 4 U** is £20
   plus a daily rate. Work out the daily rate.
   Sid wants to compare the cost of hiring a car from
   Cars 4 U and from **Car Co** who charge £25 for
   each day of hire. Sid hires cars for different periods
   of time. He wants to use the cheaper company.
   c Which of these two companies is the cheaper to
   hire the car from? You must show your working
   and explain your answer.

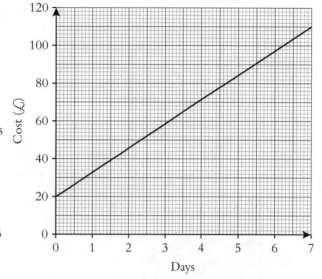

2 On a coordinate grid with values of x from -3 to $+3$
   and values of y from -6 to $+8$, draw the graph of
   $y = 2x + 1$

3 Find the equations of the two straight lines **a** and **b**.

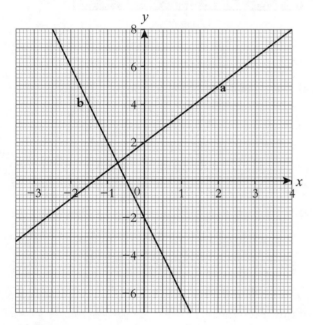

4 Here is the graph of $y = x^2 - 4x + 3$
   a Write down the minimum value of y.
   b Find the points where the line $x + y = 4$ crosses the curve.

5 The line l has a gradient of 2 and passes through $(2, -3)$.
   a Find the equation of the straight line l.
   b Explain whether or not the point $(3, -1)$ lies on the line l.

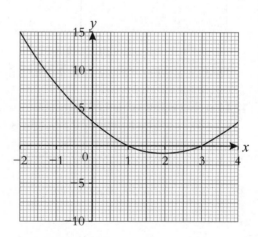

6 A quadratic function passes through the points (2, 0) and (0, 4). The function has only got one root.

   a Sketch the graph of the function.

   b Find an equation of the function.

7 The cost, C, pence per mile of the fuel used to run a car travelling at v miles per hour is given by the formula $C = \frac{v}{10} + \frac{50}{v}$

   a Sketch the graph of the function for values of v for $0 < v \leqslant 60$ mph.

   b Estimate the minimum cost per mile.

8 Alison is x years old.

  Alison is 2 years older than Bethany.

  Cathy is twice as old as Bethany.

  The total of their ages is 50.

  What is Cathy's age?

9 The perimeter of the triangle is 24 cm. The perimeter of the rectangle is 40 cm.

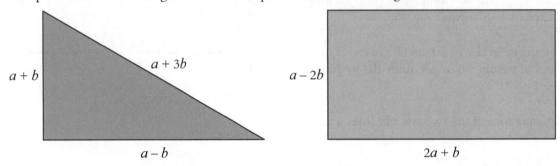

  Find the areas of the two shapes.

10 Find graphically the vertices of the triangle formed by the straight lines with equations:

$$x + y = 5 \qquad y = 2x + 3 \qquad 2y = x - 3$$

11 The rectangle has an area of $x^2 - 12x + 32$

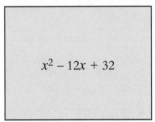

  Find an algebraic expression for the length and width of this rectangle.

12 Here is a right-angled triangle area 30 cm². The length of the base is $(x + 4)$ cm. The length of the height is $(x - 3)$ cm. Work out the perimeter of the triangle.

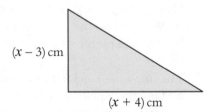

Geometry and Measures: pre-revision check

Check how well you know each topic by answering these questions. If you get a question wrong, go to the page number in brackets to revise that topic.

1 The bearing of A from B is 235°.
  a Draw the bearing of A from B.
  b Use your diagram to work out the bearing of B from A.   (page 59)

2 A plan of a garden design is drawn to a scale of 1 : 25. The total length of fencing shown on the plan is 68 cm.
  a How many metres of fencing will be needed for the actual garden? The actual lawn will be 3.5 m wide.
  b How wide will the lawn be on the diagram? (page 59)

3 A slug moves at a speed of 1.2 cm/sec. How far will the slug have moved in 2 hours? Give your answer in metres.   (page 60)

4 The density of platinum is 21.4 g/cm³. A wedding ring has a volume of 0.7 cm³. Calculate the mass of the ring.   (page 61)

5 Name the quadrilaterals that have   (page 62)
  a one pair of opposite sides parallel
  b four equal sides
  c rotational symmetry order 2.

6 Write down the size of angles a and b.   (page 63)

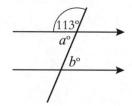

7 Work out the size of the exterior and interior angles of a regular 12-sided polygon.   (page 64)

8 Which two of the following triangles are congruent? Give a reason for your answer. (page 65)

9 Explain why all equilateral triangles are always similar but not all equilateral triangles are congruent.   (page 66)

10 Find the area and circumference of a circle with a radius of 5 cm.   (page 67)

11 Find the length of the side marked x in this right-angled triangle.   (page 68)

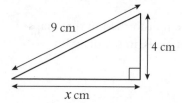

12 AOB is a sector of a circle with radius 7 cm. The angle AOB is 120°.
  a Calculate the arc length of the sector AOB.
  b Calculate the area of the sector AOB.
  (page 69)

13 Using a ruler and pair of compasses only, construct the triangle XYZ such that XY = 8 cm, XZ = 6.5 cm and angle XYZ = 90°.   (page 72)

14 a Draw the locus of all the points 3 cm from a point A.
  b Draw the locus of all the points equidistant from a pair of parallel lines 4 cm apart.
  (page 73)

15 A rectangle is enlarged by a scale factor of 5. The lengths of the sides of the rectangle are 3 cm and 4.5 cm. Work out the lengths of the sides of the enlarged image.   (page 74)

16 Triangles A and B are similar. Calculate the value of x.   (page 76)

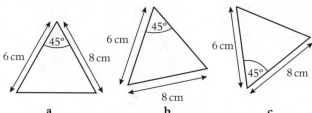

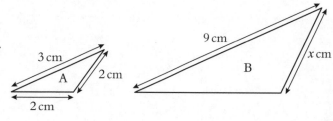

17 Work out the length of AC. (page 77)

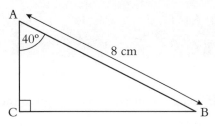

18 Calculate the exact length of AC in the triangle ABC. (page 78)

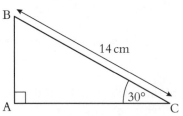

19 Describe fully the transformation that maps triangle T to triangle R in the diagram below. (page 79)

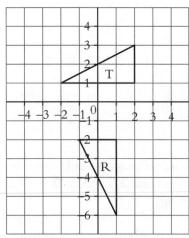

20 Sketch the nets, plan view and side elevation of
  a a cuboid
  b a right-angled triangular prism. (page 81)

21 Calculate the volume and surface area of this cuboid. (page 82)

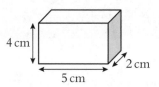

22 Calculate the volume and surface area of this cylinder. (page 82)

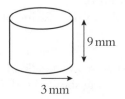

23 A cube is enlarged by a scale factor of 2. The volume of the original cube is 7 cm³. Calculate the volume of the enlarged cube. (page 84)

24 Draw the plan, front and side elevations of the object shown below. (page 81)

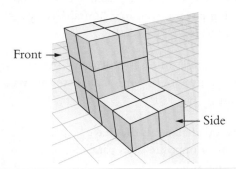

25 A pyramid has a square base with sides of 7 cm. The height of the pyramid is 10 cm. Calculate the volume of the pyramid. (page 86)

26 a Work out $\overrightarrow{AB} + \overrightarrow{BC}$
  b Draw the vector $\overrightarrow{AB} + \overrightarrow{BC}$ on a grid. (page 87)

Bearings and scale drawings

Rules

1. Bearings are always measured from North in a clockwise direction.
2. Bearings are always given using three figures.
3. A scale drawing is the same shape as the original and all its lengths are in the same ratio.
4. A scale factor is the ratio of the lengths of the original to those in the scale drawing.

Worked examples

a   B is 4 cm from A on a bearing of 100°. Draw the bearing of B from A.

Answer

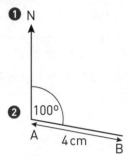

b   Daniel has a model of a house on a scale of $\frac{1}{40}$ th. The front of the model house is 0.5 m wide. The model house is 40 cm high.
    i   How wide is the real house?
    ii How high is the real house?

Answer
The real house is 40 times bigger than the model.

i   Width of real house = 40 × 0.5 m = 20 m ❹
ii Height of real house = 40 × 40 cm = 1600 cm or 16 m

Key terms

Bearing

Scale drawing

Scale factor

Ratio

Look out for

Make sure you give units with your answer.

To change cm to metres divide by 100.

Exam-style questions

1   Greenfield is a village 6 miles due East of Blackford. The village of Redham is 4 miles from Blackford and lies on a bearing of 135°.
    a   Draw a scale diagram showing the positions of the three villages. **[4]**
    b   Use your diagram to work out the bearing of Redham from Greenfield. **[2]**

2   A map has a scale of 1 : 25 000. On the map the distance between two bridges across a river is 8 cm.
    a   What is the actual distance between the two bridges? **[1]**
    b   The actual length of the river is 6.7 km. How long is the river on the map? **[1]**

3   The bearing of B from A is 080°. Work out the bearing of A from B. **[1]**

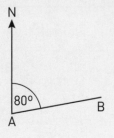

Exam tip

Draw a North line before you start.

Exam tips

Use Rule ❸.

Check your answer is realistic.

Compound units

Rules

❶ A compound measure involves two quantities, for example speed is measured in distance and time.

❷ In a compound unit 'per' means 'for each' or 'for every'.

❸ If you need to change the units of a compound unit change one quantity at a time.

Key terms

Speed

Per

Rate

Worked examples

a Galston runs 300 m in 30 s. Work out his average speed in

   i   metres per second
   ii km per min.

Answer

$$\text{average speed} = \frac{\text{distance}}{\text{time}} \text{ ❶}$$

  i   Galston's average speed $= \frac{300\,m}{30\,s}$

$$= 10 \text{ metres per second}$$

  ii $10 \times 60 = 600$ metres per minute ❸
$$= 600 \div 1000 \text{ km per min} = 0.6 \text{ km per min}$$

b A car uses petrol at the rate of 8 km per litre.
How much petrol would the car use for a journey of 300 km.

Answer

Amount of petrol used $= \frac{300}{8} = 37.5$ litres ❷

Look out for

To change m to km divide by 1000.

To change seconds to minutes divide by 60.

You can use '/' instead of per.

Remember

Don't forget to include units in your answer.

Exam-style questions

1 The distance from London to Larnaca in Cyprus is 3212 km. A plane takes 3 hours and 30 mins to fly from London to Larnaca.

   Work out the average speed of the plane. **[2]**

2 There are 50 litres of water in a barrel. The water flows out of the barrel at a rate of 125 millilitres per second (1 litre = 1000 millilitres).

   Work out the time taken for the barrel to empty completely. **[3]**

3 Sarab and Julian both drive their own cars from London to Leeds. Sarab's car averages 10 km per litre of petrol, and uses 32 litres of petrol for the drive to Leeds. Julian's car averages 5 km per litre of petrol for the same drive.

   Work out the number of litres Julian's car needs for the drive. **[4]**

Exam tip

When you answer questions involving changing units make sure your final answer is sensible.

Working with compound units

Rules

❶ A compound measure involves two quantities, for example
speed = distance ÷ time
❷ In a compound unit 'per' means 'for each' or 'for every'.
❸ If you need to change the units of a compound unit change one
quantity at a time.
❹ Density is a compound unit.
Density = mass ÷ volume

Worked examples

a The volume of a silver bar is 50 g.
The density of silver is 10.5 g/cm³.
Work out the mass of the silver bar.

Answer
Density = mass ÷ volume ❹
Density × volume = mass (make mass the subject of the formula) ❶
Mass of bar is 10.5 × 50 = 525 g

b A cheetah can run at 33 m/s

i How long would the cheetah take to run a km?
ii Work out the cheetah's speed in km/h.

Answer
i Time = distance ÷ speed ❷
= 1000 ÷ 33 = 30.3 s
ii Speed = 0.033 m/s (change m to km divide by 1000) ❸
0.033 × 3600 = 119 km/h 3 s.f. (multiply by 3600 to change from
seconds to hours)

Key terms

Rate of change

Speed

Density

Population density

Mass

Unit price

Look out for

Remember to change the
units.

Exam-style questions

1 The area of Costa Rica is 51 100 km².
In 2013 the population of Costa Rica was 4.87 million. In 2015 the
population of Costa Rica was 5.06 million.

Calculate the change in population density of Costa Rica between
2013 and 2015. **[2]**

2 An iron nail has a volume of 0.9 cm³ and a mass of 7 g.
a Calculate the density of iron. **[1]**
b An iron girder has a volume of 1.5 m³.
Calculate the mass of the girder in kg. **[1]**

3 A motorway traffic sign indicates that it is 13 mins to the next
junction on the motorway.
The junction is 14 miles away.

What assumption has been made about the speed of the traffic? **[3]**

Exam tips

Population density is a
compound measure so the
units for your answer should
include two quantities.

Make sure you show all the
stages of your working.

CHECKED ANSWERS ☐

Types of quadrilateral

Rules

❶ A quadrilateral has 4 sides.
❷ The 4 angles of a quadrilateral add up to 360°.

Worked examples

a Draw a parallelogram, showing its properties.

Answer

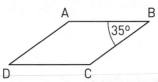

> **Exam tip**
>
> You will need to use these markings to show properties of shapes.

b Which quadrilaterals have
  i   only one pair equal sides
  ii   two pairs of equal sides
  iii   opposite sides parallel and same length.

Answer
i   trapezium
ii   square, rhombus, kite
iii   square, rectangle, parallelogram, rhombus

> **Exam tip**
>
> You will need to learn all the properties of each type of quadrilateral.

c The diagram shows a rhombus.
Work out the size of the other angles.

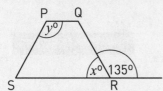

Answer
Angle D = 35° (opposite angles of a rhombus are equal)
Angle A = 180° − 35° = 145° (supplementary angles add
                                         up to 180°) ❷
Angle C = 145° (opposite angles are equal)

> **Key terms**
>
> Quadrilateral
> Square
> Rectangle
> Parallelogram
> Trapezium
> Kite
> Rhombus
> Diagonal

Exam-style questions

1 PQRS is an isosceles trapezium.
Work out the values of x and y. **[2]**

2 ABCD is a quadrilateral.
AB and CD are parallel and equal.
Angle A = Angle C. AC = 2BD.
What type of quadrilateral is ABCD? **[1]**

> **Exam tip**
>
> Draw a sketch of the quadrilateral showing its properties.

CHECKED ANSWERS

Angles and parallel lines

Rules

1. Lines that are the same distance apart are called parallel lines.
2. Corresponding angles are equal.
3. Alternate angles are equal.
4. Supplementary angles add up to 180°.
5. Vertically opposite angles are equal.

Worked examples

a Find the size of each angle marked with a letter and give a reason for each answer.

Answer
a = 57 (angles on a straight line add to 180°)

b = 57 (alternate angles are equal) ❸

c = 123 (vertically opposite angles are equal, supplementary angles add to 180°) ❺ ❹

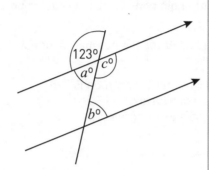

b Find the size of each angle marked with a letter.

Answer
s = 32 (32° and s are corresponding angles) ❷

t = 148 (s and t are supplementary angles) ❹

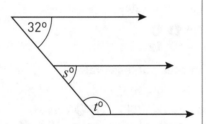

Key terms

Parallel

Corresponding

Alternate

Supplementary

Vertically opposite

Exam-style questions

1 AB is parallel to CD. Write down the values of x and y and give reasons for your answers. **[2]**

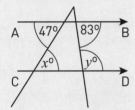

2 PQ and RS are parallel lines. Work out the value of x. **[1]**

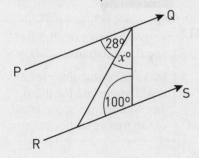

Exam tip

Make sure you give full explanations or reasons if you are asked for them.

e.g. don't just write 'alternate angles' write 'alternate angles are equal'.

Angles in a polygon

Rules

1. An interior angle is the angle inside the polygon.
2. The sum of all the interior angles of a n-sided polygon is $180(n - 2)°$
3. The exterior angle is the angle on the outside of a polygon.
4. The sum of all the exterior angles of a polygon is $360°$
5. Exterior angle + interior angle = $180°$
6. In a regular polygon all the interior angles are equal and all the exterior angles are equal.

Worked examples

a Work out the size of the exterior angle of an 18-sided regular polygon.

Answer
Exterior angle = $360° ÷ 18$ (divide $360°$ by the number of sides)
    = $20°$ ④

b The sum of the interior angles of a regular polygon is $720°$
  i How many sides does the polygon have?
  ii What is the size of the polygon's exterior angle?

Answer
i $180(n - 2) = 720$ ②

$n - 2 = \frac{720}{180}$

$n - 2 = 4$; $n = 6$, so the polygon has 6 sides.

ii exterior angle = $360° ÷ 6 = 60°$ ④ ⑥
   exterior angle = $180° - 120° = 60°$ ⑤

c Explain why a regular pentagon does not tessellate.

Answer
Sum of interior angles of a pentagon = $180(5 - 2)°$ ② = $540°$,
            therefore each interior angle = $108°$ ⑥
Regular pentagons will not tessellate as 360 cannot be divided by 108 exactly and there will be gaps formed between the shapes.

Key terms

Regular polygon
Interior angle
Exterior angle
Pentagon
Hexagon
Heptagon
Octagon
Decagon

Exam-style questions

1 The diagram shows a regular octagon and a regular pentagon joined along one edge. Calculate the value of x. **[3]**

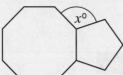

2 Sides AB, BC and CD are 3 sides of a regular n-sided polygon. Work out the values of m and n. You must give reasons for your answers. **[4]**

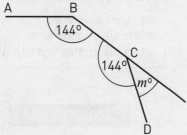

Exam tips

You need to learn the names and properties of all the regular polygons.

Make sure you give reasons if you are asked for them. You will not get some or all of the marks without them.

Congruent triangles and proof

Rules

Two triangles are congruent if one of the following conditions is true:
1. The three sides of each triangle are equal (SSS).
2. Two sides and the included angle are equal (SAS).
3. Two angles and the corresponding side are equal (AAS).
4. Each triangle contains a right angle, and the hypotenuse and another side are equal (RHS).

Worked examples

a Which of the following triangles are congruent? Give reasons for your answers.

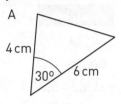 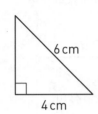

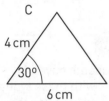 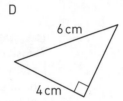

Key terms

Congruent

Proof

Answer

A and C are similar; two sides and the included angle are equal. ❷

B and D are congruent, they are right-angled triangles and the hypotenuses and one other side are equal. ❹

b PQRS is a rhombus. Prove that triangles PQX and RSX are congruent.

Answer

PQ = RS, all sides of a rhombus are equal.

PX = XR and SX = XQ, diagonals of a rhombus bisect each other. ❶

So triangles PQX and RSX are congruent (SSS).

Exam tip

Make sure you know all the conditions for congruency.

Exam tip

Make sure you finish your proof with a conclusion.

Exam-style questions

1 ABC is an equilateral triangle. X and Y are the midpoints of sides AB and BC. Prove that AYC and AXC are congruent triangles. **[3]**

2 PQRS is a parallelogram. X is the midpoint of PQ. Y is the midpoint of RS. Prove XQS and QYS are congruent. **[3]**

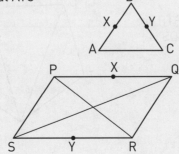

Exam tip

Only use the properties given in the question in your answer

Proof using similar and congruent triangles

Rules

❶ Shapes are similar if one is an enlargement of the other.

Two triangles are congruent if one of the following conditions is true:
❷ The three sides of each triangle are equal (SSS).
❸ Two sides and the included angle are equal (SAS).
❹ Two angles and the corresponding side are equal (AAS).
❺ Each triangle contains a right angle, and the hypotenuse and another side are equal (RHS).

Worked examples

a Which of the following triangles are similar? Give reasons for your answers.

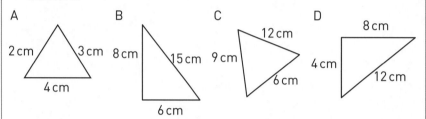

Key terms

Similar

Congruent

SSS, SAS, ASA, RHS

Answer
A and C are similar, the lengths of the sides of triangle C are all three times the lengths of the sides of triangle A. ❶

b Prove that triangles WXY and WZY are congruent.

Answer
WY is the hypotenuse of both triangles. WX = ZY (given); angles WZY and WXY are right angles (given); so WXY and WZY are congruent (RHS). ❺

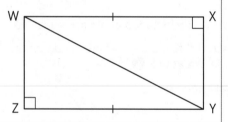

Exam tip

Many students have problems with these types of questions because they have not learnt the rules for congruent triangles.

Exam-style questions

1 Prove that triangles AXD and BXC are similar. **[3]**

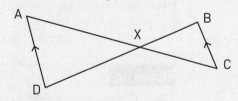

Exam tips

The only properties you can use to prove congruency or similarity are those given in the question.

Make sure you show every step of your reasoning.

2 PQRST is a regular pentagon. Prove that triangles QRS and STP are congruent, hence prove that PQS is an isosceles triangle. **[5]**

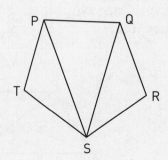

Circumference and area of circles

Rules

1. The circumference of a circle, C, with a diameter d is $C = \pi d$
2. The circumference of a circle, C, with a radius r is $C = 2\pi r$
3. π has an approximate value of 3.14 or you can use the π button on your calculator.
4. The area of a circle, A, with a radius r is $A = \pi r^2$

Worked examples

a Find **i** the area **ii** the circumference
of a circle with a diameter of 6 cm.

Answer

i $C = \pi d$ ❶
$C = \pi \times 6$
$C = 18.849$ ❸ (use the π
    button on your calculator)
$C = 18.85$ cm to 2 d.p.

ii $A = \pi r^2$ ❷
$A = \pi \times 3 \times 3$
$A = 28.27$
$A = 28.27$ cm to 2 d.p.

b Find the diameter of a circle with a circumference of 25 mm.

Answer
$C = \pi d$ ❶
$C \div \pi = d$
$25 \div \pi = d$ (divide both sides by π)
$7.957 = d$
$d = 7.96$ mm to 3 s.f.

c Find the perimeter, p, and area, A, of this shape.

Answer
perimeter of the shape $= \frac{3}{4} \times 2\pi r + 2r$
$p = (0.75 \times 2 \times \pi \times 4) + (2 \times 4)$
$p = 18.849... + 8$
$p = 26.85$ cm to 2 d.p.
$A = \frac{3}{4} \pi r^2$
$A = \frac{3}{4} \times \pi \times 4 \times 4$
$A = 37.7$ cm² to 3 s.f.

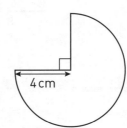

4 cm

Key terms

Circumference

Diameter

Radius

Pi

π

Perimeter

Exam tips

Always write down the unrounded value from your calculator before rounding.

Give answer to 3 s.f. unless you are told otherwise.

Exam tips

Always show all stages of your working.

Do not forget to include units in your answer.

Exam-style questions

1. A wheel barrow has a front wheel with a diameter of 20 cm.
A gardener uses the wheelbarrow to move some soil 50 m.
How many times will the front wheel rotate during the move? **[3]**

2. The diagram shows a window. The window
is made from a rectangle and a semicircle.
The perimeter of the window is 30 m.
   a Calculate the value of x.
   b Calculate the area of the window. **[4]**

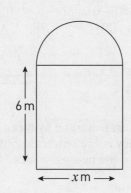

6 m

x m

CHECKED ANSWERS

Pythagoras' theorem

Rules

1. Pythagoras' theorem can be written as $a^2 + b^2 = h^2$, where h is the hypotenuse of a right-angled triangle and a and b are the other sides of the triangle.
2. To find h add the squares of each of the other sides together and then square root the answer.
3. To find a or b subtract the square of the known side from the square of the hypotenuse and square root the answer.

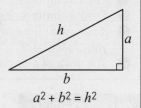

$a^2 + b^2 = h^2$

Worked examples

a ABC is a right-angled triangle.
Find the length of side AB to 1 d.p.

Answer
$AB^2 = AC^2 + CB^2$ (AB is hypotenuse) ❶ ❷

$AB^2 = 9^2 + 7^2$

$AB^2 = 81 + 49$

$AB = \sqrt{130}$ (use the square root button
             to find $\sqrt{130}$)

$AB = 11.4$ cm to 1 d.p.

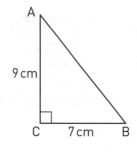

b Find the value of x.

Answer
$x^2 = 12.3^2 - 8.5^2$ (x is a smaller side) ❸

$x^2 = 151.29 - 72.25$

$x = \sqrt{79.04}$

$x = 8.9$ cm to 1 d.p.

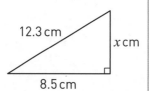

Key terms

Right-angled triangle

Pythagoras

Hypotenuse

Square

Square root

Look out for

Make sure you write down all the steps in your working.

Exam tip

The hypotenuse of a right-angled triangle is the longest side. Always identify the hypotenuse before you start answering the question.

Exam-style questions

1 PQR is an isosceles triangle.
PQ = PR = 8 cm
QR = 5 cm

Calculate the vertical height of the triangle PQR, give your answer to 1 d.p. **[3]**

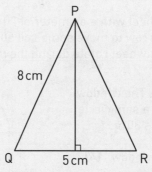

Exam tip

Draw a diagram of the course and mark it with the information given to you in the question.

2 Sally sails a yacht around a course marked by three coloured buoys. The red buoy is 700 metres east of the blue buoy. The green buoy is 1500 metres south of the blue buoy. Calculate the total length of the course. Give your answer to the nearest metre. **[3]**

Arcs and sectors

Rules

For a sector with angle $\theta°$ of a circle and radius r:

❶ the area of the sector is $\frac{\theta}{360} \times \pi r^2$

❷ the length of the arc is $\frac{\theta}{360} \times \pi d$ or $\frac{\theta}{360} \times 2\pi r$

Worked examples

a i Find the area.

   ii Find the arc length of the shaded sector.

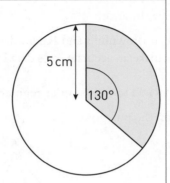

Answer

i area of the sector = $\frac{\theta}{360} \times \pi r^2$ **❶**

     = $\frac{130}{360} \times \pi \times 5^2$

     = 28.4 cm² to 2 d.p.

ii arc length = $\frac{\theta}{360} \times 2\pi r$ **❷**

     = $\frac{130}{360} \times 2 \times \pi \times 5$

     = 11.3 cm to 2 d.p.

b A sector of a circle with radius 6 cm has an arc length of 8 cm. Find the angle of the centre of the sector to the nearest degree.

Answer

arc length = $\frac{\theta}{360} \times 2\pi r$

   8 = $\frac{130}{360} \times 2 \times \pi \times 6$

  2880 = $12\pi x$

2880 ÷ $12\pi = x$, so the angle at the centre = 76° to nearest degree.

Exam-style questions

1 The diagram shows a sector of a circle, centre O.
The radius of the circle is 9 cm.
Angle POQ is 80°.
Work out the perimeter of the sector to the nearest cm. **[4]**

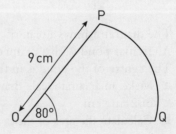

2 The diagram shows the design for a pendant.

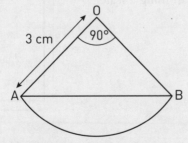

The pendant is made from a gold isosceles triangle joined to a silver segment to form a sector.
The finished pendant is a sector AOB radius 3 cm with a centre angle of 90°. Calculate the area of the silver part of the pendant. **[5]**

CHECKED ANSWERS ☐

Mixed exam-style questions

1 The diagram show the position of two villages.
   Redford is on a bearing of 050° from Brownhills.
   Karen walks from Brownhills to Redford.
   She walks at an average speed of 6 km/h.
   She takes 1 h 30 mins to cover the distance.

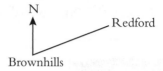

    a Work out the distance between Brownhills and Redford. **[2]**

    b Using a scale of 1 cm to 4 km, make an accurate scale drawing showing the position of the two villages. **[3]**

2 The diagram shows a square attached to four similar regular polygons.

  Calculate the number of sides on the polygons. **[3]**

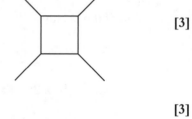

3 ABC is an isosceles triangle.
   D and E are points on BC.
   AB = AC, BD = EC
   Prove that triangle ADE is isosceles. **[3]**

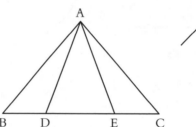

4 The wheel on a bicycle has a diameter of 70 cm.
   John cycles 15 km on the bicycle.

    a How many revolutions will the wheel make during the journey? **[4]**

    b The journey takes John 1 h 20 mins. Calculate John's average speed. **[2]**

5 In the diagram PQ is parallel to ST.
   QX = XS

  Prove that triangles PQX and STX are congruent.

6 The diagram shows a plan of a garden design.
   A circular pond with a diameter of 1.5 m is dug in the lawn.
   The centre of the pond is in the centre of the lawn.

    a Make an accurate scale drawing of the plan using a scale of 2 cm : 1 m **[4]**

    b Calculate the area of the lawn. **[4]**

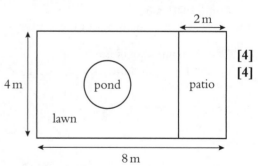

7 The diagram shows a right-angled triangle drawn inside a quarter circle.
The chord AC is 3 cm.

   a Calculate the radius of the circle.   **[3]**

   b Calculate the area of the segment ABC.   **[4]**

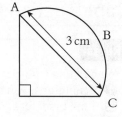

8 A paper cone is made from a folding a piece of paper in the shape of
the sector of a circle. The angle at the centre of the sector is 100°.
The radius of the sector is 6 cm.

   a Calculate the length of the arc of the sector.   **[2]**

   b Calculate the diameter of the base of the finished cone.   **[2]**

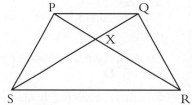

9 The diagram shows a trapezium PQRS.
PQ is parallel to SR.
PS = QR
Show that triangles PXS and QXR are similar.   **[3]**

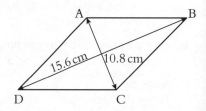

10 ABCD is a rhombus.
AC = 10.8 cm, BD = 15.6 cm
Calculate the length of the sides of the rhombus.   **[4]**

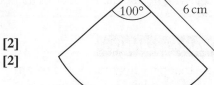

Constructions with a pair of compasses

Rules

You can use a pair of compasses and ruler to construct the following:
1. Triangles given their sides
2. Line bisectors
3. Angle bisectors
4. The perpendicular from a point to a line

Worked examples

a   Using a ruler, pencil and pair of compasses make an accurate drawing of the triangle ABC.

Answer
Draw the line AB 6.7 cm using a ruler.

Construct a perpendicular at point B. ❹

Construct a perpendicular at point A. ❹

Bisect the angle at A. ❸

Extend the angle bisector from A and the perpendicular at B until they meet at C.

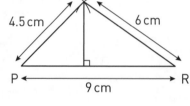

b   Using a ruler and pair of compasses, make an accurate drawing of PQR.

Answer
Draw the line PQ 9 cm using a ruler. ❶

Use a pair of compasses 4.5 cm wide at P to draw an arc at Q.

Use a pair of compasses 6 cm wide at R to draw an arc to intersect at Q.

Draw the lines PQ and RQ.

Construct the perpendicular from Q to PR. ❹

Exam tips

Read the question carefully to check what equipment you may use.

You must show all your construction lines, **do not** rub them out.

Key terms

Arc

Bisector

Perpendicular

Look out for

Make sure all your measurements are very accurate; angles within 2° and lengths within 1 mm. You will lose marks for inaccuracy.

Exam-style questions

1   a   Using a ruler, pencil and pair of compasses, make an accurate drawing of the triangle ABC. **[3]**
    The line AX bisects the angle BAC.
    b   Construct the line AX. **[2]**
    c   Measure the distance BX. **[1]**

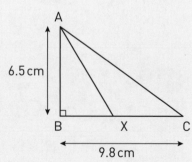

2   Using a ruler, pencil and pair of compasses construct the triangle XYZ such that XY = 9 cm, YZ = 6.5 cm and XZ = 7 cm. **[3]**

3   a   Draw a horizontal line PQ 9 cm long and using a pair of compasses only, construct the perpendicular bisector of the line PQ. Mark the point X where that the bisector crosses the line PQ. **[2]**
    b   Mark the point S on the perpendicular bisector so that SX = 5.7 cm. **[1]**
    c   Measure the angle SPQ. **[1]**

CHECKED ANSWERS

Loci

HIGH

Rules

❶ A locus is a line or a curve that joins all the points that obey a given rule.

Some of the most common loci are:
❷ A constant distance from a fixed point
❸ Equidistant from two given points
❹ A constant distance from a given line
❺ Equidistant from two lines

Worked examples

a Draw the locus of all the points that are equidistant from two points, A and B, which are 5 cm apart.

Answer

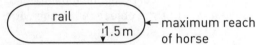

The locus is the perpendicular bisector of the line joining A and B. ❶ ❸

b A horse is tethered by a rope to a straight rail 10 m long. The rope is 1.5 m long. The horse can walk around both sides of the rail. Make a sketch of locus of the maximum reach of the horse. ❶ ❹

Answer

Key terms

Locus

Loci

Equidistant

Exam-style questions

1 The position of two mobile phone masts A and B are shown. The signal from mast A can reach 10 km. The signal from mast B can reach 7 km.
Using a scale of 1 cm to 2 km, draw an accurate diagram to show the region covered by both masts. **[3]**

15 km

A   B

2 XYZ is a triangle.
XY = YZ = 8 cm
XZ = 6 cm

Mark the point x that is equidistant from X, Y and Z. **[4]**

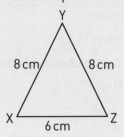

Exam tips

If you are asked to draw an accurate diagram, you should use a ruler and/or compass to construct the loci.

You should leave all the construction marks.

Remember

Do not forget to make it clear to the examiner where the final region required is by shading and labelling it.

CHECKED ANSWERS

Enlargement

Rules

1. Enlargements are described using a scale factor and centre of enlargement.
2. The scale factor is the amount a shape has been enlarged and can be found by dividing the length of a side of the image by the length of the corresponding side of the object.
3. If the image is smaller than the object the scale factor for the enlargement will be a fraction.

Worked examples

a Plot the points A(2,1), B(4,4), C(5,2) on a set of axes. Join the points to form a triangle. **1** Enlarge the triangle by a scale factor of 2, using (0,0) as the centre of enlargement. Label the points of your image A′ B′ C′.

Answer

b Describe fully the transformation that maps shape A on to shape B.

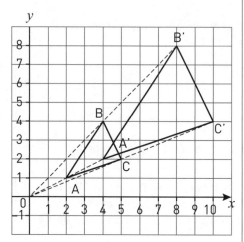

Exam tip

When you are asked to perform an enlargement, make sure that corresponding sides are parallel.

Answer

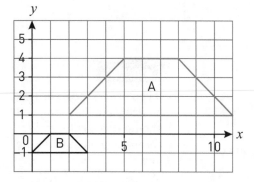

Remember

To find the **centre of enlargement,** join the corresponding points of the object and image with straight lines.

The centre of enlargement is where all the lines cross.

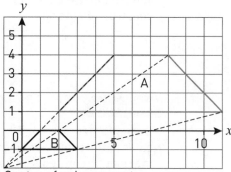

Centre of enlargement

Enlargement, scale factor = $3 \div 9 = \frac{1}{3}$ **2** **3**

Centre of enlargement = (–1, –2)

Key terms

Object

Image

Scale factor

Centre of enlargement

Map

1 Describe fully the transformation that maps shape A on to B. **[2]**

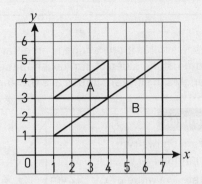

2 Copy the diagram.
Enlarge the shape Q with a scale factor of $\frac{1}{2}$.
Centre of enlargement is (0,0).
Label your answer P.

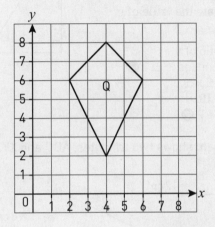

CHECKED ANSWERS

Similarity

Rules

1. Shapes are similar if one shape is an enlargement of the other.
2. The lengths of the sides of similar shapes are in the same ratio.
3. All the angles in similar shapes are the same.

Worked examples

a The diagram shows two similar triangles.

  i Calculate the value of x.
  ii Calculate the value of y.

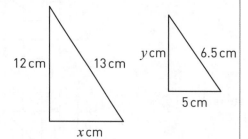

Answer

  i The ratio of the hypotenuses is $2:1$ ❷
  So $x = 2 \times 5$
  $x = 10$

  ii $y = 12 \div 2$ ❷
  $y = 6$

b The diagram shows two triangles, ABC and XYZ. Find the size of angle XZY.

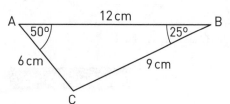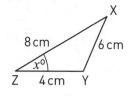

Answer

The corresponding sides of triangles ABC and XYZ are in the same ratio. ❶ ❷

Therefore triangles ABC and XYZ are similar triangles. Angle XZY corresponds to angle BAC. ❸

So $x = 50$

Key terms

Similar

Ratio

Remember

You can work out the ratio by dividing the lengths of corresponding sides.

Look out for

When answering questions on similar shapes, make sure you use the ratio of corresponding sides.

Exam-style questions

1. The diagram shows triangle ABC.
   Angle BAC = 37°
   AC = 10.5 cm, BC = 7 cm
   YC = 4.5 cm
   The line XY is parallel to the line BC.

   Calculate the length of the line XY. **[3]**

2. PQ is parallel to SR.
   QP = 8 cm
   SR = 10 cm
   PX = 6 cm

   Calculate the length of PS. **[3]**

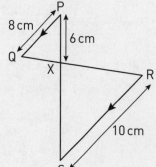

Trigonometry

Rules

For a right-angled triangle:

1 $\tan\theta = \frac{\text{opposite}}{\text{adjacent}}$

2 $\sin\theta = \frac{\text{opposite}}{\text{hypotenuse}}$

3 $\cos\theta = \frac{\text{adjacent}}{\text{hypotenuse}}$

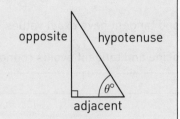

Key terms

Sine

Cosine

Tangent

Worked examples

a ABC is a right-angled triangle.

Work out the size of angle ACB to 1 d.p.

Answer

$\cos B = \frac{8.6}{13.7}$ **3**

$\cos B = 0.6277$

$ACB = 51.1°$ (Use the inverse cos on your calculator).

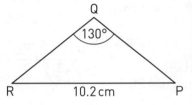

b PQR is an isosceles triangle.

Angle PQR = 130°, QR = PQ

PR = 10.2 cm

Calculate the length of QR to 1 d.p.

Answer

As PQR is isosceles, RXQ is a right-angled triangle.

RX = 5.1 cm, RQX = 65°

$\sin 65° = \frac{5.1}{QR}$ **2**

$QR = \frac{5.1}{\sin 65°}$

$QR = 5.63$ cm

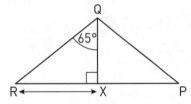

Look out for

Although you use a calculator for these problems, you still need to show the stages of your working.

Exam tip

It is often helpful to mark new information on a diagram, or even draw a new one.

Exam-style questions

1 A ladder is placed against a wall.
The foot of the ladder is 1.2 m away from the wall.
The top of the ladder is placed 3 m up the wall.
a Calculate the angle the ladder makes with the wall. **[2]**
b Calculate the length of the ladder. **[2]**

2 PQRS is a square.
The length of each side of the square is 8 cm.

Use trigonometry to calculate the length of the diagonal, PR. **[3]**

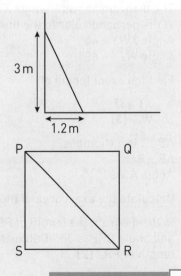

Trigonometry for special angles

Rules

❶ Some values of sine, cosine and tangent have exact values, these can be used to give exact answers to questions.

❷ Using exact values of sine, cosine and tangent avoids rounding errors.

Worked examples

a The diagram shows triangle ABC.

AB = 8 cm

Angle ABC = 30°

Calculate the exact value of

Answer

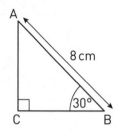

i AC

$$\sin 30° = \frac{AC}{8}$$

$$\frac{1}{2} = \frac{AC}{8}$$

$$AC = 4 \text{ cm}$$

ii BC

$$\cos 30° = \frac{BC}{8}$$

$$\frac{\sqrt{3}}{2} = \frac{BC}{8}$$

$$\frac{8\sqrt{3}}{2} = BC$$

$$BC = 4\sqrt{3} \text{ cm}$$

b In the triangle PQR, PQ = 9 cm, angle QPR = 30°

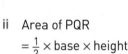

i Calculate the exact length of QR.

ii Calculate the exact area of triangle PQR.

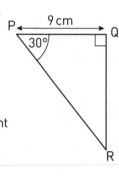

Answer

i $\tan 30° = \frac{QR}{9}$

$$\frac{1}{\sqrt{3}} = \frac{QR}{9} \ ❶$$

$$\frac{9\sqrt{3}}{3} = QR$$

$$QR = 3\sqrt{3} \text{ cm}$$

ii Area of PQR

$$= \frac{1}{2} \times \text{base} \times \text{height}$$

$$= \frac{1}{2} \times 9 \times 3\sqrt{3} \ ❷$$

$$= \frac{27\sqrt{3}}{2} \text{ cm}^2$$

Key values you need to learn

$$\sin 45° = \cos 45° = \frac{1}{\sqrt{2}}$$

$$\sin 30° = \cos 60° = \frac{1}{2}$$

$$\sin 60° = \cos 30° = \frac{\sqrt{3}}{2}$$

$$\sin 90° = 1$$

$$\cos 90° = 0$$

$$\tan 45° = 1$$

$$\tan 30° = \frac{1}{\sqrt{3}}$$

$$\tan 60° = \sqrt{3}$$

Exam tip

When simplifying your answers remember:

$$\frac{1}{\sqrt{2}} = \frac{\sqrt{2}}{2}$$

$$\frac{1}{\sqrt{3}} = \frac{\sqrt{3}}{3}$$

This topic will usually appear on the non-calculator paper.

Exam-style questions

1 The diagram shows triangle XWZ, WY is perpendicular to the line XZ.

Angle XWY = 45°

Angle WZY = 60°

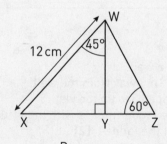

Find the exact length of

a XY **[3]**

b WZ **[3]**

2 ABCD is a rhombus.

AB = 8 cm

Angle A = 60°

Calculate the exact area of the rhombus. **[4]**

3 In the diagram the length of PQ is 5 √3 cm and angle QRP is 30°. Calculate the exact length of PR. **[2]**

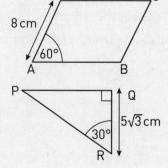

Finding centres of rotation

Rules

❶ To describe a rotation fully you need to state the direction, angle and centre of rotation.
❷ The centre of rotation is where the perpendicular bisectors of the lines that join the corresponding points of the image and object cross.

Worked examples

a Describe the rotation that maps

  i   A → B
  ii A → C
  iii A → D

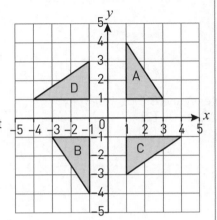

Answer

  i   180° clockwise rotation about (0,0) ❶
  ii 90° clockwise rotation about (0,0) ❶
  iii 90° anti-clockwise rotation about (0,0) ❶

b Image P has been rotated to form image Q.

  i   Find the centre of rotation that maps P to Q.
  ii Describe fully the transformation.

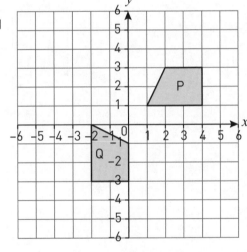

Answer

  i   Centre of rotation is (–1,2) ❶
  ii 180° clockwise rotation about (–1,2) ❷

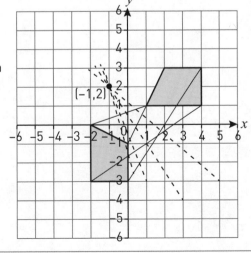

Key terms

Transformation

Rotation

Centre of rotation

Clockwise

Anti-clockwise

Exam tip

You should leave the lines you used to find the centre of rotation in your answer, as you may get some marks for them if you make a mistake later.

Look out for

Don't forget to write down your answer after finding the centre of rotation.

Exam-style questions

1 Quadrilateral A has been rotated to position B.
  a Find the centre of rotation that maps quadrilateral A to quadrilateral B. **[2]**
  b Describe fully the transformation that maps quadrilateral A to quadrilateral B. **[2]**

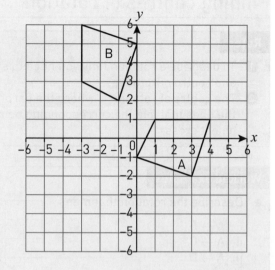

2 The diagram shows two triangles A and B. Describe fully the transformation that maps A onto B. **[2]**

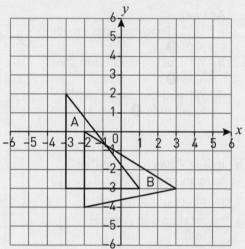

CHECKED ANSWERS

Understanding nets and 2D representation of 3D shapes

Rules

1. 2D nets can be folded to make hollow 3D shapes.
2. A plan of a 3D shape is the view from above.
3. An elevation of a 3D shape is the view from the front or side.
4. Isometric paper can be used to make accurate drawings of 3D shapes.

Worked examples

a Make a sketch of the net of this cylinder.

Answer
The net of a cylinder is made from a rectangle and 2 circles. ①

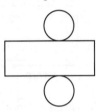

b On squared paper draw the plan and front elevation of the shape shown below. ④

Answer

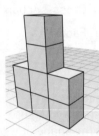

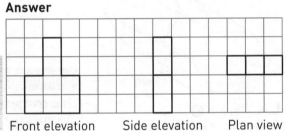

Front elevation   Side elevation   Plan view

 ③   ②

Key terms

Net

2D shape

3D shape

Elevation

Plan view

Isometric

Exam tip

It would be useful to learn the shapes of the nets of a cuboid, pyramid, prism and cylinder.

Look out for

Isometric paper should be the right way up, with vertical lines and no horizontal lines.

Exam-style questions

1 The plan view, front and side elevations for a prism are shown below. On isometric paper draw a 3D representation of the prism. **[3]**

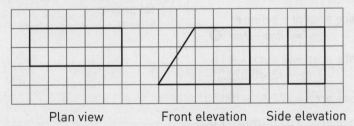

Plan view   Front elevation   Side elevation

2 The diagram shows a square-based pyramid. Make an accurate drawing of the net of the pyramid. **[5]**

Look out for

If you are asked to make an accurate drawing of a net, you will need to use a ruler and/or pair of compasses.

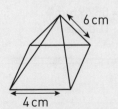

6 cm

4 cm

Volume and surface area of cuboids and prisms

Rules

1. Volume of a cuboid = length × width × height
2. Surface area of a cuboid = 2 × (area of base + area of one side + area of front)
3. Volume of a prism = area of cross section × height (or length)
4. Surface area of a prism = total area of all the faces
5. Volume of a cylinder = $\pi r^2 h$
6. Surface area of a cylinder = $2\pi rh + 2\pi r^2$

Worked examples

a Work out the volume and surface area of this cuboid.

Answer

Volume = length × width × height ❶

Volume = 8 × 4 × 6

Volume = 192 cm³

Surface area = 2 × (area of base + area of side + area of front) ❷

Surface area = 2 × ((8 × 4) + (4 × 6) + (8 × 6))

Surface area = 2 × (32 + 24 + 48)

Surface area = 208 cm²

b The diagram shows a prism with a hexagonal cross-section. The area of the cross-section is 36 cm². Calculate the volume of the prism.

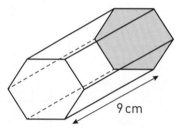

Answer

Volume of a prism = area of cross section × length ❸

Volume = 36 × 9 = 324 cm³

c A cylinder has a radius of 4 mm and length 11 mm. Workout the volume and surface area of the cylinder.

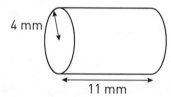

Answer

Volume of a cylinder
  = $\pi r^2 h$ ❺

Volume = $\pi \times 4 \times 4 \times 11$

Volume = 552.9 mm²
  (1 d.p.)

Surface area of a cylinder
  = $2\pi rh + 2\pi r^2$ ❻

Surface area = (2 × π × 4 × 11) + (2 × 50.26...)

Surface area = 274.6...+ 100.53

Surface area = 377.0 mm³ (1 d.p)

Exam tip

Don't forget to include units in your answers.

Key terms

Volume

Surface area

Prism

Cross-section

Faces

Remember

The **cross-section** of a prism is the shape you get when you cut the shape at right angles to its length.

Look out for

When you use a calculator to work out problems do not round your answers until the final answer.

Exam-style questions

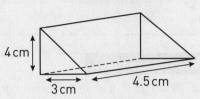

1 A cylindrical water tank has a radius of 2.5 m and a height of 5 m.
   a   Calculate the volume of the tank. **[3]**
   b   Workout the maximum amount of water the tank can hold in litres. **[2]**

2 The diagram shows a triangular prism. The cross-section of the prism is
  a right-angled triangle.
   a   Calculate the area of the cross-section of the prism. **[2]**
   b   Calculate the volume of the prism. **[1]**
   c   Calculate the surface area of the prism. **[3]**

3 A manufacturer makes stock cubes. The stock cubes are made
  in 2 cm cubes. She wants to sell the cubes in boxes of 12 and they
  will be packed with no spaces.
  Work out the dimensions of all the possible boxes the manufacturer could choose from. **[3]**

CHECKED ANSWERS

Enlargement in two and three dimensions

Rules

❶ If the ratio of lengths of similar shapes is $1 : x$, the ratio of their areas is $1 : x^2$

❷ If the ratio of lengths of similar shapes is $1 : x$, the ratio of their volumes is $1 : x^3$

Worked examples

a Triangle P is an enlargement of triangle Q. The area of triangle Q is $3\,\text{cm}^2$. Calculate the area of triangle P.

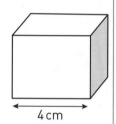

Answer

Ratio of sides = 2 : 6 or 1 : 3

Ratio of area = $1 : 3^2$ or 1 : 9 ❶

Area of triangle P = $9 \times 3\,\text{cm}^2$

$= 27\,\text{cm}^2$

b The diagram shows two cuboids. The volume of the larger cuboid is $64\,\text{cm}^3$. Calculate the volume of the smaller cuboid.

Answer

Ratio of sides = 2:4 or 1:2

Ratio of volumes = $1:2^3$ or 1:8 ❷

Volume of the smaller cuboid = $64\,\text{cm}^3 \div 8$

$= 8\,\text{cm}^3$

Exam tip

You should always reduce ratios to their simplest form when answering this type of question.

Key term

Ratio

Look out for

As you are finding the volume of the smaller shape, you need to divide by 8 to find the answer.

Exam-style questions

1 The two crosses in the diagram are mathematically similar. The area of the smaller shape is $90\,\text{cm}^2$.

  a Calculate the area of the larger shape. **[2]**

The crosses are cross-sections of two mathematically similar prisms.

  b Write down the ratio of their volumes. **[1]**

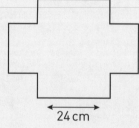

2 A manufacturer makes metal toy cars in two different sizes. The large car is an enlargement of the small car. The small car is 5 cm long and the large car 7.5 cm long. It takes $16\,\text{cm}^3$ of metal to make the small car.

Calculate the volume of metal required to make the large car. **[3]**

3 The diagram shows two cones. Cone B is an enlargement of A. The radius of the base of cone A is 2 cm. The area of the base of cone B is 6 times larger than the area of cone A.

Calculate the radius of the base of cone B. **[3]**

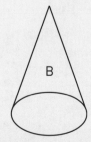

Constructing plans and elevations

REVISED ☐

HIGH

Rules

❶ Isometric drawings are used to accurately represent 3D objects
❷ In Isometric drawings vertical edges are drawn vertically, horizontal edges are drawn slanted.
❸ A plan of a 3D shape is the view from above.
❹ An elevation of a 3D shape is the view from the front or side.

Key terms

Plan

Elevation

Isometric

Worked examples

a Make an isometric drawing from these elevations and plan. ❶ ❷

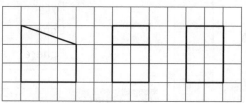

Front elevation Side elevation Plan

Answer

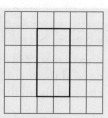

Front

Side

Look out for

Make sure the isometric paper is the right way up!

b Draw the plan, front and side elevations of this 3D shape. ❸ ❹

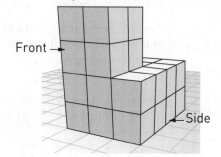

Front

Side

Answer

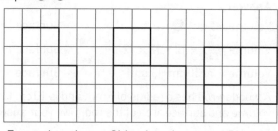

Front elevation   Side elevation   Plan

Exam tips

You should label the front and side of a 3D drawing.

You should clearly identify which diagram is the plan or elevation.

Exam-style questions

1 Make an isometric drawing of the shape that has these elevations and plan.   **[3]**

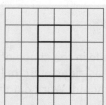
Front elevation   Side elevation   Plan

2 Draw the plan, front and side elevations of

a

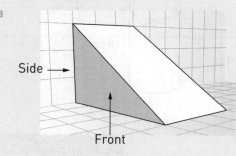

Side →

Front

[3]

b

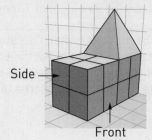

Side →

Front

[3]

CHECKED ANSWERS ☐

Surface area and 3D shapes

Rules

1. Volume of a pyramid = $\frac{1}{3}$ base area × height
2. Volume of a cone = $\frac{1}{3}\pi r^2 h$
3. Volume of a cylinder = $\pi r^2 h$
4. Surface area of a cylinder = $2\pi rh + 2\pi r^2$
5. Volume of a sphere = $\frac{4}{3}\pi r^3$
6. Surface area of a sphere = $4\pi r^2$

Key terms

Surface area

Pyramid

Cone

Sphere

Worked examples

a A cone has a radius of 4 cm and a height of 9 cm. Work out the volume of the cone. Give your answer in terms of π.

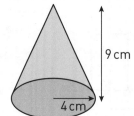

9 cm

4 cm

Answer

Volume of a cone = $\frac{1}{3}\pi r^2 h$ **2**

Volume = $\frac{1}{3} \times \pi \times 4 \times 4 \times 9$

Volume = 48π cm^3

b A basket ball has a diameter of 24 cm. Calculate the volume and surface area of the basketball.

Answer

Volume = $\frac{4}{3}\pi r^3$ **5**

Volume = $\frac{4}{3}\pi \times 12 \times 12 \times 12$

Volume = 7230 cm^3 (3 s.f.)

Surface area = $4\pi r^2$ **6**

Surface area = $4 \times \pi \times 12 \times 12$

Surface area = 1810 cm^2 (3 s.f.)

c A wooden rod has a radius of 6 mm and is 10 cm long. Calculate the volume and surface area of the rod. Give your answer to 1 decimal place.

Answer

Volume of a cylinder = $\pi r^2 h$ **3**

Volume = $\pi \times 0.6 \times 0.6 \times 10$

Volume = 11.3 cm^3 (1 d.p.)

Surface area of a cylinder
= $2\pi rl + 2\pi r^2$ **4**

Surface area = $2\pi \times 0.6 \times 10 +$
$2\pi \times 0.6 \times 0.6$

Surface area = 39.0 cm^2 (1 d.p.)

Look out for

Make sure you read the question carefully, e.g. in this question you are told the diameter but the formulae requires the radius.

Always give your answers to at least 3 significant figures if not told the accuracy required.

Sometimes the units are mixed, change all lengths to the same units.

Exam tip

Students often get this type of question wrong because they do not change the measurements to the same units.

Exam-style questions

1 A cake mould is made in the shape of a square-based pyramid. The base of the mould has sides of 5 cm. It takes 50 cm^3 of cake mixture to completely fill the mould. Work out the height of the cake mould. **[4]**

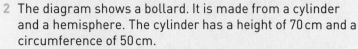

5 cm

2 The diagram shows a bollard. It is made from a cylinder and a hemisphere. The cylinder has a height of 70 cm and a circumference of 50 cm.

a The bollard is going to be made of metal. Calculate the total volume of metal required to make the bollard. **[6]**

b All exposed surfaces of the finished bollard will be painted white. Calculate the total surface area to be painted. **[4]**

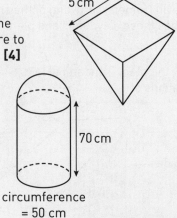

70 cm

circumference = 50 cm

Vectors

Rules

1. A vector has magnitude and direction.
2. Vectors can be written in three different ways.
3. Vectors can be added, subtracted or multiplied by a scalar.

Worked examples

a $\overrightarrow{AB} = \begin{pmatrix} 4 \\ 3 \end{pmatrix}$, $\overrightarrow{BC} = \begin{pmatrix} 3 \\ -2 \end{pmatrix}$

   i Draw vectors $\overrightarrow{AB}$ and $\overrightarrow{BC}$ on a grid.

   ii Write down the column vector for $\overrightarrow{AB} + \overrightarrow{BC}$.

Answer

i

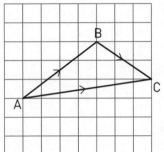

❶

ii $\overrightarrow{AB} + \overrightarrow{BC}$ is the vector joining A to C, $\overrightarrow{AC}$

$\overrightarrow{AC} = \begin{pmatrix} 7 \\ 1 \end{pmatrix}$

b Work out these vector computations.

   i $\begin{pmatrix} 4 \\ 3 \end{pmatrix} + \begin{pmatrix} 2 \\ -1 \end{pmatrix}$ **ii** $\begin{pmatrix} 6 \\ 4 \end{pmatrix} - \begin{pmatrix} -4 \\ 2 \end{pmatrix}$ **iii** $2\begin{pmatrix} 3 \\ 4 \end{pmatrix}$

Answer

i $\begin{pmatrix} 4 \\ 3 \end{pmatrix} + \begin{pmatrix} 2 \\ -1 \end{pmatrix} = \begin{pmatrix} 4+2 \\ 3+-1 \end{pmatrix} = \begin{pmatrix} 6 \\ 2 \end{pmatrix}$

ii $\begin{pmatrix} 6 \\ 4 \end{pmatrix} - \begin{pmatrix} -4 \\ 2 \end{pmatrix} = \begin{pmatrix} 6--4 \\ 4-2 \end{pmatrix} = \begin{pmatrix} 10 \\ 2 \end{pmatrix}$

iii $2\begin{pmatrix} 3 \\ 4 \end{pmatrix} = \begin{pmatrix} 3 \times 2 \\ 4 \times 2 \end{pmatrix} = \begin{pmatrix} 6 \\ 8 \end{pmatrix}$

c Draw a diagram on squared paper to show the following vector addition.

$\begin{pmatrix} 3 \\ 2 \end{pmatrix} + \begin{pmatrix} 4 \\ -4 \end{pmatrix}$

❷

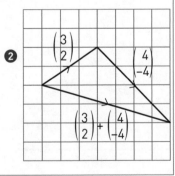

Key facts

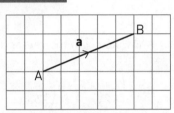

The vector from A to B can be written as: $\overrightarrow{AB}$

$\mathbf{a} = \begin{pmatrix} 5 \\ 2 \end{pmatrix}$ (column vector)

Key terms

Vector

Scalar

Column vector

Exam tip

Students often lose marks on these questions because they forget the rules for adding and subtracting negative numbers.

Exam-style questions

1 $\mathbf{a} = \begin{pmatrix} 4 \\ -2 \end{pmatrix}$ $\mathbf{b} = \begin{pmatrix} 3 \\ 2 \end{pmatrix}$ $\mathbf{c} = \begin{pmatrix} -1 \\ 6 \end{pmatrix}$

   a Work out
      i $\mathbf{a} + \mathbf{b}$
      ii $\mathbf{b} - \mathbf{c}$
      iii $2\mathbf{b}$
      iv $2\mathbf{a} + 3\mathbf{b}$ **[4]**

   b On a grid show the following vectors.
      i $\mathbf{b} + \mathbf{c}$
      ii $2\mathbf{b}$ **[2]**

2 a Write down as a column vector
      i $\overrightarrow{PQ}$

      ii $\overrightarrow{QR}$ **[2]**

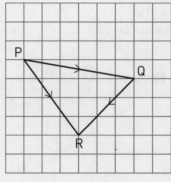

   b Write down the vector addition represented by the vector $\overrightarrow{PR}$.   **[1]**

3 $\overrightarrow{AB} = \begin{pmatrix} 4 \\ -2 \end{pmatrix}$; $\overrightarrow{CD} = \begin{pmatrix} 12 \\ -6 \end{pmatrix}$

Write down two facts about the relationship between $\overrightarrow{AB}$ and $\overrightarrow{CD}$.   **[2]**

CHECKED ANSWERS

Mixed exam-style questions

1 A ship sails on a bearing of 030° for 11.8 km.
  Calculate exactly how far east the ship is from its starting point. **[3]**

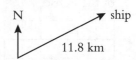

2 An isosceles triangle, ABC, has a base, AC, of 8 cm. The perpendicular height of the triangle is 5 cm.
  a Using a ruler and pair of compasses make an accurate drawing of the triangle. **[4]**
  b Measure angle BAC on your drawing. **[1]**

3 A steel ball-bearing has a diameter of 8 mm. The density of the steel
  the ball-bearing is made from is 7.8 g/cm³.
  Calculate the mass of the ball bearing. **[3]**

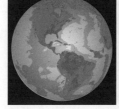

4 The diameter of the moon is 3474 km.
  The diameter of the earth is 12 742 km.
  Work out the ratio of the surface areas of the moon and
  the earth.
  Give your answer in the form 1 : *x*. **[3]**

5 A triangular prism has a cross-section in the shape of an equilateral
  triangle. The sides of the triangle are 9 cm. The prism is 15 cm long.
  a Calculate the area of the cross-section. **[4]**
  b Calculate the volume of the prism. **[2]**
  A smaller version of the prism is mathematically similar to the
  original. The length of the new prism is 5 cm.
  c Calculate the area of the cross-section of the new prism. **[2]**
  d Calculate the surface area of the new prism. **[3]**

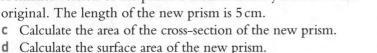

6 A harbour has two rocks at its entrance. The distance between the
  rocks is 900 m. In order to enter the harbour safely a ship must sail at
  the same distance from each rock.
  Using a scale of 1 cm to 150 m, draw an accurate diagram to show the
  safe route of the ship. **[3]**

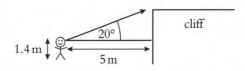

7 Penny is standing at 5 m from the foot of a cliff. She sees the top
  of the cliff at an angle of elevation of 20°. Penny's eye is 1.4 m
  above the ground.
  Work out the height of the cliff.

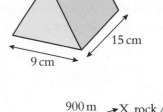

8 A pyramid has a square base of 4 cm. The edges of the pyramid are
  6 cm long.
  a Using ruler and pair of compasses only, make an accurate drawing
  of the net of the pyramid. **[4]**
  b Using measurements taken from your drawing, work out the
  surface area of the pyramid. **[4]**

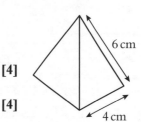

9 A water tank is made in the shape of a cylinder. The cylinder is 1.3 m high and has a radius of 40 cm. The tank is filled with water at the rate of 20 litres/min.
Calculate the time taken to completely fill the water tank.   **[5]**

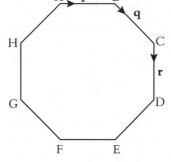

10 The plan, front and side elevations of a house are shown below. Make an isometric drawing of the house.   **[3]**

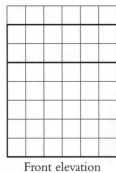
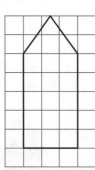
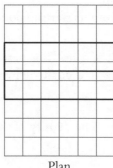

Front elevation   Side elevation   Plan

11 ABCDEFGH is a regular octagon. $\overrightarrow{AB} = \mathbf{p}$

  a Explain why $\overrightarrow{EF} = \mathbf{p}$ **[1]**

  $\overrightarrow{BC} = \mathbf{q}; \overrightarrow{CD} = \mathbf{r}$

  b Find $\overrightarrow{AC}$ **[1]**

  c Find $\overrightarrow{AD}$ **[1]**

  d Write down $\overrightarrow{FH}$ **[1]**

12 Describe fully the transformation that will map shape A onto B.   **[2]**

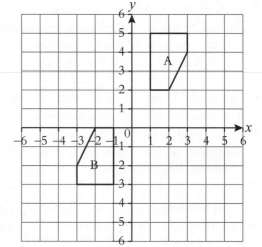

Statistics and Probability: pre-revision check

Check how well you know each topic by answering these questions.
If you get a question wrong, go to the page number in brackets to revise that topic.

1 Charlie recorded the number of goals scored in each of 20 games of football. Here are her results.

Number of goals	1	2	3	4	5
Frequency	5	7	4	2	2

  a Find the median number of goals scored.
  b Work out the mean number of goals scored per game. (page 93)

2 Hattie has a shop. The table gives information about the amount of money spent by each of 60 people in Hattie's shop.

Amount spent ($£x$)	$0 < x \leqslant 5$	$5 < x \leqslant 10$	$10 < x \leqslant 15$	$15 < x \leqslant 20$	$20 < x \leqslant 25$
Frequency	3	6	19	25	7

  a In which group does the median lie?
  b Work out an estimate for the mean amount spent. (page 95)

3 The table gives information about the number of people living in a village from 1950 to 2010.

Year	1950	1960	1970	1980	1990	2000	2010
Number of people	90	80	100	110	190	240	280

  a Draw a vertical line graph to show the information in the table.
  b Work out the percentage increase in the number of people living in the village between 1980 and 1990.
  c Describe the trend. (page 96)

4 The table gives some information about the ages of the 54 people on a coach tour.

Age group (in years)	under 20	20 to 39	over 39
Frequency	18	24	12

Lara is going to draw a pie chart to show this information. Work out the angle she should use for the under 20 age group. (page 97)

5 Here are the times taken, in seconds, for some students to do an arithmetic test.

19	26	28	33	27	29
33	31	31	17	32	23
23	20	22	27	28	34

Make a grouped frequency table for this data using intervals $10 < x \leqslant 20$, $20 < x \leqslant 30$, and so on. (page 98)

6 The table gives information about the age and the trunk radius of each of eight trees. (page 100)

Age (years)	26	42	50	33	55	58	36	48
Trunk radius (cm)	14	30	42	22	44	52	22	34

a Draw a scatter diagram to show this information.

b Describe and interpret the correlation shown in your scatter diagram.

Another tree has an age of 65 years.

c i Find an estimate for the trunk radius of this tree.

ii How reliable is your estimate? Explain why.

7 Here are some letter tiles.

A	A	A	B	B	C	X

Naomi is going to take at random one of these tiles.

a What is the probability that Naomi will take the letter A?

b What is the probability that Naomi will **not** take the letter B?
(page 104)

8 Mary spins a 4-sided spinner and a 3-sided spinner. Her score is the difference of the two numbers on the spinners, as shown in the table. (page 105)

a Find the probability that Mary's score is 0.

b Find the probability that Mary's score is greater than 1.

		3-sided spinner		
		1	2	3
4-sided spinner	1	0	1	2
	2	1	0	1
	3	2	1	0
	4	3	2	1

9 Jay spins a 3-sided spinner 20 times. Here are her results.
(page 106)

Number	1	2	3
Frequency	9	3	8

Jay is going to spin the spinner one more time.

a Write down an estimate for the probability that the spinner will land on 2.

b Jay thinks the spinner is biased. Is she right? Give a reason for your answer.

10 There are four blue counters and two yellow counters in a bag. Terri is going to take two counters at random from the bag. Work out the probability that both counters will be the same colour. (page 107)

11 In a survey of 50 people, 35 people said they like semi-skimmed milk, 40 people said they like skimmed milk and 28 people said they like both.

a Draw a Venn diagram to show this information.

b One of these people is taken at random. Work out the probability that this person does not like semi-skimmed milk or skimmed milk. (page 109)

Using frequency tables

Rules

1. The mode is the most common value.
2. The median is the middle value when the data is in order of size.

   The middle value is the $\frac{n+1}{2}$ th value.
3. The range is the difference between the largest and smallest values.
4. To calculate the mean from a frequency table add a $f \times x$ column and a total row to the table.
5. The mean is the sum of all the $f \times x$ values divided by the number of values. Mean $= \frac{\Sigma f \times x}{n}$

Worked example

In a survey 21 people were asked how many loaves of bread they each bought in a week. The table gives information about the results.

Number of loaves (x)	Frequency (f)	$f \times x$
0	4	$0 \times 4 = 0$
1	7	$1 \times 7 = 7$
2	9	$2 \times 9 = 18$
3	1	$3 \times 1 = 3$
Total	21	28

Work out

  i the mode   ii the median   iii the mean   iv the range.

Answer

  i Mode = 2 **1** The most common value is the value with the highest frequency. The highest frequency is 9, so the mode is 2

  ii Median = 1 **2** The middle value is the $\frac{21+1}{2} = \frac{22}{2} = 11$th value

     There are four 0s, seven 1s, nine 2s, etc., so the 11th value is 1

  iii Add a $f \times x$ column and a Total row to the table. **4**

     Mean $= \frac{28}{21} = 1.33$ (2 d.p.) **5** The sum of all the $f \times x$ values is 28

     The number of values is 20, so the mean = 28 ÷ 21 = 1.33...

  iv Range = 3 **3** The largest value is 3, the smallest value is 0, so 3 – 0 = 3

Key term

Frequency

Exam tips

1. Remember that multiplying any number by 0 equals 0
2. If the size of the sample is given in the question (21 in this case) check that the total frequency is equal to it.
3. Give your answers to an appropriate degree of accuracy, generally 3 significant figures or at least 2 decimal places.

1 Mary asks 25 people at a dog show how many dogs they each own. Here are her results.

Number of dogs (x)	Frequency (f)
1	9
2	7
3	5
4	3
5	1

Work out
a   the mode **[1]**
b   the median **[1]**
c   the mean **[3]**
d   the range. **[2]**

2 Satbir asked some people how many times they each went to the cinema in the last month. The table shows information about her results.

Number of times (x)	Frequency (f)
0	11
1	15
2	9
3	5

Work out
a   the mode **[1]**
b   the median **[1]**
c   the mean **[3]**
d   the range. **[2]**

CHECKED ANSWERS

Using grouped frequency tables

Rules

1 The modal group is the group with the highest frequency.

2 The median is the middle value when the data is in order of size.

The middle value is the $\frac{n+1}{2}$ th value.

3 To calculate the mean from a grouped frequency table you need to add a mid-interval value column, a $f \times x$ column, and a total row to the table.

4 The estimated mean is the sum of all the $f \times x$ values divided by the number of values. Mean $= \frac{\Sigma f \times x}{n}$

Worked example

The table gives information about the heights of some children.

Height (x cm)	Frequency (f)	Mid-interval value	$f \times x$
$130 < x \leqslant 140$	10	135	$10 \times 135 = 1350$
$140 < x \leqslant 150$	16	145	$16 \times 145 = 2320$
$150 < x \leqslant 160$	17	155	$17 \times 155 = 2635$
$160 < x \leqslant 170$	7	165	$7 \times 165 = 1155$
Total	**50**		7460

Key terms

Frequency

Mid-interval value

Exam tip

Give the units with your answer.

i Write down the modal group.

ii Find the group that contains the median height.

iii Work out an estimate for the mean height.

Answer

i The modal group is $150 < x \leqslant 160$ **1**. The group with the highest frequency (17) is $150 < x \leqslant 160$, so this is the modal group.

ii The group that contains the median height is $140 < x \leqslant 150$ **2**. The middle value of the data is the $\frac{50+1}{2}$th = 25.5th value, i.e. half way between the 25th and 26th values. There are 10 values in the group $130 < x \leqslant 140$ and 16 values in the group $140 < x \leqslant 150$, so both the 25th and 26th values appear in the group $140 < x \leqslant 150$, so the median value is in the group $140 < x \leqslant 150$.

iii Add a mid-interval value column, a $f \times x$ column, and a total row to the table **3**. Mean $= \frac{7460}{50} =$ 149.2 cm **4**. The sum of all the $f \times x$ values is 7460, the number of values is 50, so the estimated mean is $7460 \div 50 = 149.2$

Exam-style questions

1 The table shows information about the time taken, in seconds, for each of 70 people to complete a logic problem.

Time taken (x seconds)	Frequency (f)
$30 < x \leqslant 40$	5
$40 < x \leqslant 50$	8
$50 < x \leqslant 60$	12
$60 < x \leqslant 70$	28
$70 < x \leqslant 80$	17

Work out an estimate for the mean time taken. **[4]**

2 Jai recorded the weights, in kg, of some packages. His results are summarised in the table.

Weight (w kg)	Frequency (f)
$1 < w \leqslant 1.5$	29
$1.5 < w \leqslant 2$	17
$2 < w \leqslant 2.5$	11
$2.5 < w \leqslant 3$	8

a Write down the modal group. **[1]**

b Find the group that contains the median weight. **[1]**

c Work out an estimate for the mean weight. **[4]**

CHECKED ANSWERS

Vertical line charts

Rules

1. The scales on the axes do not need to be the same as each other.
2. The scale must be the same along each axis so that the numbers are evenly spaced.
3. If time is involved it goes along the horizontal axis.
4. Label the axes and give the chart a title.

Worked example

The table gives the average highest temperatures recorded in Manchester each month in 2015.

Month	J	F	M	A	M	J	J	A	S	O	N	D
Temp (°C)	6	6	9	12	15	18	20	20	17	14	9	7

Key term

Trend

i   Draw a vertical line chart to show this information.
ii Which two months had the highest average temperatures?
iii Describe the shape of the distribution.

Answer

i

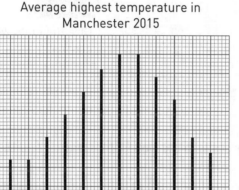

Average highest temperature in Manchester 2015

Exam tip

Be extra careful when interpreting the scale on the vertical axis. Sometimes one square does not represent one unit.

ii The highest average temperatures are given by the tallest lines. The tallest lines are July and August.
iii Average highest temperatures increased from their lowest values in winter, to their highest values in summer, and then decreased again in autumn.

Exam-style questions

1   Fiona sells umbrellas in a shop. The table shows the number of umbrellas she sold each day one week in April.

Day	Mon	Tue	Wed	Thu	Fri	Sat	Sun
Frequency	8	3	4	15	9	6	6

a   Draw a vertical line chart to show this information. **[3]**
b   Fiona sold more umbrellas on Thursday than on any other day. Suggest a reason why. **[1]**
c   The cost of each umbrella is £5.99. How much money did Fiona get for selling umbrellas that week? **[2]**

2   Pam rolled a dice 30 times. Here are her results.

6, 5, 1, 4, 2, 6, 5, 6, 6, 2, 3, 6, 5, 3, 3, 4, 5, 6, 6, 6, 4, 3, 2, 4, 5, 2, 4, 6, 9, 2

a   Draw a vertical line chart to show this information. **[3]**
b   Pam says the dice is biased. Do you agree? Explain why. **[1]**

CHECKED ANSWERS

Pie charts

Rules

1. To draw a pie chart from a frequency table you need to add a 'sector angle' row to the table.
2. The total frequency (n) is the sum of all the frequencies.

3. The angle needed for one item is $\frac{360}{n}$, where n is the total frequency.

4. To calculate the sector angle you multiply the sector frequency (f) by the angle needed for one item: $f \times \frac{360}{n}$

5. To calculate the sector frequency you divide the sector angle (A) by 360 and multiply by the total frequency (n): $\frac{A}{360} \times n$

Worked examples

a The table shows the number of votes Pierre, Carlos, Sasha and Evelyn each got in an election. Draw a pie chart to show this information.

	Pierre	Carlos	Sasha	Evelyn
Number of votes	18	24	33	15
Sector angle	72°	96°	132°	60°

Answer

Add a 'sector angle' row to the table ①. The total frequency (n) = 18 + 24 + 33 + 15 = 90 ②. Angle needed for one vote = $\frac{360}{90} = 4°$ ③.

Sector angle for Pierre = 18 × 4 = 72°
Sector angle for Carlos = 24 × 4 = 96°
Sector angle for Sasha = 33 × 4 = 132°
Sector angle for Evelyn = 15 × 4 = 60° ④

Draw the pie chart.

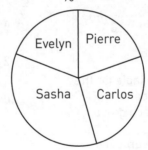

Exam tips

Check your calculations of the sector angles by adding them all up. The total should be 360°.

Label the sectors of your pie chart.

Use a protractor to draw the angles of the pie chart accurately.

Key terms

Sector angle

Sector frequency

b The pie chart shows information about the weights of the ingredients needed to make a cake. Kerry uses the information in the pie chart to make a cake. The weight of the cake is 900 grams. How much butter did Kerry use?

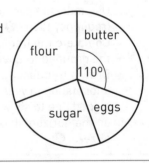

Answer

The sector angle (A) is 110, the total frequency (n) is 900, so
$\frac{110}{360} \times 900 = 275$ grams ⑤

Exam-style questions

1 The table shows some information about the drinks sold in a shop one day. Draw a pie chart to show this information. **[4]**

Drink	Tea	Coffee	Juice	Cola
Frequency	12	8	27	25

2 Tony uses the information in the pie chart in Worked example b above to make a cake. He has 385 grams of butter and plenty of the other ingredients. Work out the weight of the largest cake Tony can make. **[2]**

Statistics and Probability

Rules

1. Use groups of equal width when drawing a frequency diagram.
2. Tallies are used to record data in the appropriate groups.
3. Complete the frequency column in the grouped frequency table by totalling tallies.
4. A jagged line is used to show that the scale on an axis does not start at zero.

Worked examples

24 students entered a high jump competition. Here is the best height, h metres, jumped by each student.

1.1	1.4	1.3	1.3	1.6	1.1	1.5	1.3	1.1	1.4	1.2	1.5
1.5	1.3	1.6	1.2	1.3	1.8	1.7	1.3	1.7	1.5	1.9	1.3

i   Display the information in a grouped frequency table. Use the groups $1 < h \leq 1.2$, $1.2 < h \leq 1.4$, and so on.
ii Draw a frequency diagram to show the data.
iii Describe the shape of the distribution.

Answer

i

Height (h metres)	Tally	Frequency
$1 < h \leq 1.2$	IIII	5
$1.2 < h \leq 1.4$	IIII IIII	9
$1.4 < h \leq 1.6$	IIII I	6
$1.6 < h \leq 1.8$	III	3
$1.8 < h \leq 2$	I	1

Draw a grouped frequency table for the information. Continue the pattern of the groups. The width of each group is equal to 0.2 metres. ❶
Use tallies to complete the grouped frequency table. ❷
Complete the frequency column in the grouped frequency table. ❸
Draw a frequency diagram for the information in your table. Use a jagged line to show that the scale on the horizontal axis does not start at zero. ❹

ii

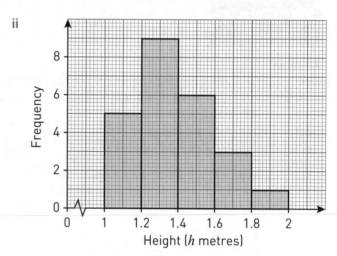

iii The modal group is $1.2 < h \leq 1.4$. The distribution is not symmetrical. The model group is on the left of the distribution so it is positively skewed.

Exam-style questions

Franz recorded the time taken, t seconds, for each of 25 telephone calls. Here are his results.

20.6	5.7	20.1	11.2	25.8	13.7	26.8	27.9	14.6	24.3	21.7	25.2	18.1
16.9	24.6	22.8	21.9	19.6	26.7	23.7	18.4	17.0	28.4	29.5	22.3	

a   Time taken is an example of continuous data. Explain why. **[1]**

b   Display the information in a grouped frequency table. Use the groups $5 < t \leqslant 10$, $10 < t \leqslant 15$, and so on. **[3]**

c   Draw a frequency diagram to show the data. **[3]**

d   Franz says that the group that contains the median time taken is the same group as the modal group. Is he right? Explain why. **[2]**

CHECKED ANSWERS

Scatter diagrams and using lines of best fit

Rules

1. An outlier is data that does not fit the pattern of the rest of the data.
2. Positive correlation is when both variables increase together.
3. Negative correlation is when one variable decreases when the other variable increases.
4. When there is correlation between the variables you can draw a line of best fit on the scatter diagram.
5. The line of best fit is the straight line that best represents the data.
6. Use a line of best fit to estimate unknown values.

Worked example

The scatter diagram shows information about the age and the mileage of a sample of 8 cars.

There is an outlier in the data.

  i Write down the coordinates of the outlier.
  ii Describe any correlation between the age and the mileage of these cars.
  iii Draw a line of best fit on the scatter diagram.
  iv A different car has an age of 4 years. Use your line of best fit to estimate the mileage of this car. Comment on the reliability of your estimate.

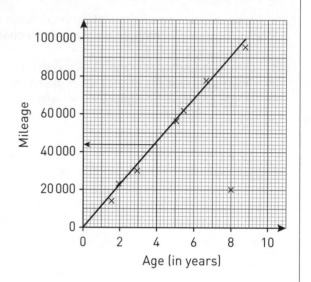

Answer

  i The data that does not fit the pattern of the other data is (8, 20 000). ❶
  ii The data shows positive correlation, the greater the age of the car the greater the mileage. ❷
  iii See scatter diagram. ❹ ❺
  iv The coordinates of the point on the line of best fit that corresponds to an age of 4 years is (4, 44 000). So an estimate for the unknown mileage is 44 000. ❻ This estimate uses interpolation. Interpolation is more reliable than extrapolation but, as the sample size is small, the estimate may be unreliable over all.

Exam tips

Show your working for estimates by drawing lines to your line of best fit when reading off values.

Be careful when interpreting scales on the axes of scatter diagrams. One square on the grid does not always represent one unit in the data.

Key terms

Bivariate data

Correlation

Interpolation

Extrapolation

Causation

A scientist recorded the sea temperature at each of eight depths. The table shows information about the results.

Depth (m)	300	150	0	250	400	450	200	100
Sea temperature (°C)	11	15.5	20	13.5	10	8	14	18

a Draw a scatter graph for this information. **[3]**

b Describe the correlation. **[1]**

c i Estimate the sea temperature at a depth of 350 metres.

   ii Estimate the depth for a sea temperature of 0 °C. Comment
       on the reliability of your estimates. **[4]**

CHECKED ANSWERS

Mixed exam-style questions

1 Jose recorded the number of sales he made on his internet shop on each of 40 days. The vertical line chart shows information about his results.

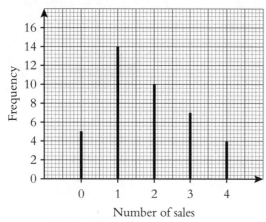

a Copy and complete the table using the information in the chart. **[2]**

Number of sales	0	1	2	3	4
Frequency					

b Find the
  i mode
  ii median
  iii mean of the data. **[5]**

c Which average do you think represents the data best?
  Give a reason for your answer. **[2]**

2 The table gives information about the birth weights of a sample of babies.

Weight (w kg)	$2 < w \leqslant 2.5$	$2.5 < w \leqslant 3$	$3 < w \leqslant 3.5$	$3.5 < w \leqslant 4$	$4 < w \leqslant 4.5$
Frequency	5	9	17	11	6

a How many babies are there in the sample? **[1]**
b Find
  i the modal group
  ii the group that contains the median weight. **[2]**
c Find an estimate for
  i the mean weight
  ii the range of the weights of the babies. **[6]**
d Explain why your answers in part **c** are only estimates. **[1]**

3 Omar recorded the number of calls to a call centre on each of 5 days. Here are his results.

Day	Mon	Tue	Wed	Thu	Fri
Number of calls	3	5	7	12	18

  a Draw
    i a vertical line chart
    ii a pie chart for this information.   **[6]**
  b Which diagram do you find the most helpful?
    Give a reason for your answer.   **[1]**

4 Emma plays noughts and crosses with her friends.

She wins $\frac{3}{5}$ of her games,

loses $\frac{1}{4}$ of her games

and draws the rest.

Draw a pie chart to show this information.   **[3]**

5 Haley is going to pick at random a letter from the word STATISTICS.
Write down the probability that the letter will be S.   **[1]**

6 The probability that Mark will get a blue paper hat in a Christmas cracker is 0.85.
Work out the probability he will not get a blue paper hat in the Christmas cracker.   **[2]**

7 In a survey, 30 people were asked if they speak French or German. Of these,
11 said they speak only French,
8 said they speak both French and German
and 4 said they speak neither French nor German.
  a Draw a Venn diagram to show this information.   **[3]**
  b One of these people is picked at random. Find the probability that this person speaks only German.   **[2]**

Single event probability

Rules

❶ P(event happening) = $\frac{\text{total number of successful outcomes}}{\text{total number of possible outcomes}}$

❷ P(event not happening) = 1 − P(event happening)

Worked examples

a A letter is going to be picked at random from the word MISSISSIPPI. Find the probability that the letter

  i will be an S

  ii will not be an S.

Answer

  i There are 4 Ss, so the total number of successful outcomes is 4 There are 11 letters altogether, so the total number of possible outcomes is 11

    P(S) = $\frac{\text{total number of successful outcomes}}{\text{total number of possible outcomes}} = \frac{4}{11}$ ❶

  ii P(not S) = 1 − P(S) = $1 - \frac{4}{11} = \frac{7}{11}$ ❷

b A bag contains some counters. Each counter has a 1, a 2, a 3 or a 4 on it. The table shows information about these counters.

Number on counter	1	2	3	4
Frequency	3	8	7	5

A counter is taken at random from the bag. Work out the probability that the counter has a number greater than 2 on it.

Answer

The total number of successful outcomes = 12, as there are 7 counters with a 3 on them and 5 counters with a 4 on them and 7 + 5 = 12

The total number of possible outcomes = 23, as the total number of counters in the bag = 3 + 8 + 7 + 5 = 23

So P(number greater than 2) = $\frac{\text{total number of successful outcomes}}{\text{total number of possible outcomes}} = \frac{12}{23}$ ❶

Exam tips

Probabilities must be written as fractions, decimals or percentages.

Do not write probabilities as a ratio.

Probabilities written as fractions need not be written in their simplest form.

Key terms

Event

Outcome

Mutually exclusive

Exam-style questions

1 A bag contains 10 counters. 3 of the counters are red the rest are green. A counter is taken at random from the bag. Write down the probability that the counter
  a will be red **[1]**   b will not be red **[2]**   c will be yellow. **[1]**

2 A weather forecaster says the probability that it will rain tomorrow is 65%.
What is the probability that it will not rain tomorrow? **[2]**

3 The sides of a 3-sided spinner are labelled A, B, and C. The probability that the spinner will land on B is twice as likely as it will land on A. The probability it will land on C is twice as likely as it will land on B. Work out the probability that the spinner will land on C. **[3]**

4 A box contains only black counters and white counters. The probability that a counter taken at random from the box will be black is $\frac{5}{12}$. There are 20 black counters in the box.
How many white counters are there in the box? **[3]**

CHECKED ANSWERS

Combined events

MEDIUM

Rules

1. Show all the possible outcomes in a list, possibility space or Venn diagram.
2. Identify all the successful outcomes.
3. P(event happening) = $\frac{\text{total number of successful outcomes}}{\text{total number of possible outcomes}}$
4. P(event not happening) = 1 – P(event happening)

Worked examples

a Giles is going to spin a 3-sided spinner numbered 1 to 3 and a 4-sided spinner numbered 1 to 4. Find the probability that the total of the two numbers on the spinners
 i will be 5 **ii** will not be 5.

Exam tips

Draw a circle around all the successful outcomes in the sample space.

There is no need to give the final answer as a fraction in its simplest form.

Answer

i Draw a sample space diagram to show all the possible outcomes. ❶

4-sided spinner

		1	2	3	4
3-sided spinner	**1**	(1, 1)	(1, 2)	(1, 3)	(1, 4)
	2	(2, 1)	(2, 2)	(2, 3)	(2, 4)
	3	(3, 1)	(3, 2)	(3, 3)	(3, 4)

Key terms

Outcome

Possibility space

Event

Sample space

Find all the successful outcomes in the sample space diagram with a total of 5, e.g. (3, 2) ❷
There are 3 successful outcomes, i.e. (3, 2), (2, 3), (1, 4)
There are 12 possible outcomes altogether.

So, P(total 5) = $\frac{\text{total number of successful outcomes}}{\text{total number of possible outcomes}} = \frac{3}{12} = \frac{1}{4}$ ❸

ii P(total not 5) = 1 – P(total 5) ❹
1 – P(total not 5) = $1 - \frac{3}{12} = \frac{9}{12} = \frac{3}{4}$

b The Venn diagram gives information about the number of people in a survey who have watched the films Cinderella (C) and Bambi (B). Some have watched both and some have watched neither. One of these people is picked at random. What is the probability that this person watched Cinderella or Bambi but not both?

Answer

The Venn diagram shows that 8 people watched only Cinderella, 5 people watched only Bambi, 3 people watched both and 6 people watched neither.
The total number of successful outcomes = 8 + 5 = 13 ❷
The total number of possible outcomes = 8 + 3 + 5 + 6 = 22
So, P(Cinderella or Bambi but not both) = $\frac{\text{total number of successful outcomes}}{\text{total number of possible outcomes}} = \frac{13}{22}$ ❸

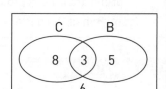

Exam-style questions

1 Tim is going to roll a 4-sided spinner numbered 1 to 4 and an ordinary 6-sided dice. Find the probability that the difference of the two numbers he gets will be 2 or less. **[3]**

2 19 people went to Tony's tea shop. Of these 19 people, 12 had a cup of a tea, 15 had a biscuit and 10 had both a cup of tea and a biscuit. One of these people is picked at random.
 What is the probability they did not have a cup of tea or a biscuit? **[4]**

CHECKED ANSWERS

Estimating probability

Rules

❶ Relative frequency gives an estimate of a probability.

❷ Relative frequency = $\frac{\text{frequency of the event}}{\text{total frequency}}$

❸ The greater the number of trials the greater the reliability of the estimated probability.

Worked examples

a A book shop does a survey to find out if people prefer their books to be hardcopy or digital. The table gives information about the results of the first 237 people surveyed.

	Hardcopy	Digital	Total
Male	59	17	76
Female	108	53	161
Total	167	70	237

Key terms

Event

Bias

Trial

Population

Sample

 i Estimate the probability that the next person to be surveyed in the book shop
  a will be male; **b** will prefer their books to be digital.
 ii Do the results show that more people prefer their books to be hardcopy than digital? Give a reason for your answer.

b Omar throws a biased dice 20 times and gets a six 5 times. Jasmine throws the same dice 150 times and gets a six 30 times. Omar and Jasmine each use their results to estimate the probability that the next time they each throw the dice it will land on six. Who has the better estimate, Omar or Jasmine? Explain why.

Answers

a i a 76 males were surveyed, so the frequency of the event is 76.
   A total of 237 people were surveyed, so the total frequency is 237.
   P(male) = $\frac{\text{frequency of the event}}{\text{total frequency}} = \frac{76}{237}$ ❶ ❷

 b 70 people in the survey prefer digital, so the frequency of the
   event is 70. A total of 237 people were surveyed, so the total
   frequency is 237. P(digital) = $\frac{\text{frequency of the event}}{\text{total frequency}} = \frac{70}{237}$ ❶ ❷

Exam tips

Probabilities must be written as fractions, decimals or percentages.

Probabilities written as fractions need not be written in their simplest form.

 ii No. The results may be biased. Hardcopies of books are sold in book shops, so there may be more people in the book shop who prefer their books to be hardcopies.

b Jasmine has the better estimate as she threw the dice more times than Omar. ❸

Exam-style questions

1 Hilary spins a biased coin 20 times. Here are her results.
 H, T, H, H, T, H, H, T, H, T, H, T, H, H, H, H, H, H, T, H
 a Find an estimate for the probability that the next time she spins the coin it will land on Heads. **[2]**
 b Hilary is going to spin the coin 300 times. Work out an estimate for the number of times the coin will land on Tails. **[2]**

2 In a survey of tourists a sample of 60 people were asked to choose to go on a Tower of London tour or on a Westminster Abbey tour. 29 males were sampled of whom 15 chose to go on the Tower of London tour. 17 females chose to go on the Westminster Abbey tour. Find an estimate for the probability that the next person to be surveyed will choose to go on the Tower of London tour. **[4]**

CHECKED ANSWERS

The multiplication rule

Rules

❶ P(A) + P(not A) = 1
❷ For independent events, P(A and B) = P(A) × P(B)
❸ For mutually exclusive events, P(A or B) = P(A) + P(B)

Worked example

There are three blue crayons and two red crayons in a box. Tina takes at random two crayons from the box.
  i Draw a tree diagram to show this situation.
  ii Work out the probability that both crayons will be the same colour.

Answers
  i Draw the tree diagram.

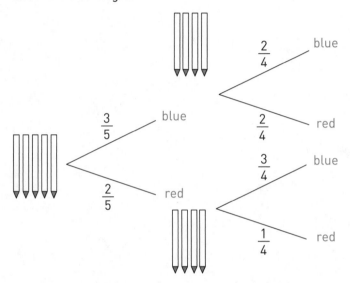

Take the crayons one at a time from the box. The colour of the first crayon affects the crayons left in the box. If the first crayon is blue there will be two blue crayons and two red crayons left in the box. If the first crayon is red, there will be three blue crayons and one red crayon left in the box.

The probabilities on each pair of branches must add to 1, as P(blue) + P(not blue, i.e. red) = 1 ❶

Key terms

Independent events

Dependent events

Mutually exclusive events

---

  ii For both crayons to be the same colour either two blue crayons are taken from the box or two red crayons are taken from the box.
The probability of taking a blue crayon first and a blue crayon second is:

P(blue first and blue second) = P(blue first) × P(blue second) = $\frac{3}{5} \times \frac{2}{4} = \frac{6}{20}$ ❷

The probability of taking a red crayon first and a red crayon second is:

P(red first and red second) = P(red first) × P(red second) = $\frac{2}{5} \times \frac{1}{4} = \frac{2}{20}$ ❷

So, the probability of taking two blue crayons or two red crayons is:
P(blue first and blue second or red first and red second) =
P(blue first and blue second) + P(red first and red second) = $\frac{6}{20} + \frac{2}{20} = \frac{8}{20} = \frac{2}{5}$ ❸

Exam hints

Multiply the probabilities 'along' the branches of the tree diagram.

Add the probabilities 'down' the branches of the tree diagram.

Leave the fractions unsimplified, including the final answer.

Exam-style questions

1 Taavi is given a raffle ticket on Wednesday and a raffle ticket on Saturday. The probability that he will win on Wednesday is 0.1. The probability that he will win on Saturday is 0.05.

   a Draw a tree diagram to show this information. **[3]**

   b Work out the probability that he will win on both days. **[2]**

   c Work out the probability that he will not win on Wednesday and win on Saturday. **[2]**

2 A bag contains three green counters and four yellow counters. A box contains one green counter and five yellow counters. Jim takes at random a counter from the box. If the counter is green Jim takes at random a counter from the bag. If the counter is yellow Jim takes another counter from the box. Find the probability that the colour of the first counter will be different to the colour of the second counter. **[5]**

CHECKED ANSWERS

The addition rule

Rules

1. P(event happening) = $\frac{\text{total number of successful outcomes}}{\text{total number of possible outcomes}}$
2. For mutually exclusive events, P(A or B) = P(A) + P(B)
3. For events that are not mutually exclusive, P(A or B) = P(A) + P(B) − P(A and B)

Worked examples

a A box contains 17 counters, of which 6 counters are black and 3 counters are white. The Venn diagram shows this information. A counter is taken at random from the box. Find the probability the counter will be
  i black
  ii white
  iii black or white.

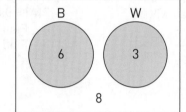

Exam tips

Write down the appropriate formula before using it.

Draw a Venn diagram to show all the information.

Answers

a i P(B) = $\frac{\text{total number of successful outcomes}}{\text{total number of possible outcomes}}$ = $\frac{6}{17}$ ❶

  ii P(W) = $\frac{\text{total number of successful outcomes}}{\text{total number of possible outcomes}}$ = $\frac{3}{17}$ ❶

  iii Taking a black counter and taking a white counter are mutually exclusive, they cannot both happen,
  so P(B or W) = P(B) + P(W); P(B or W) = $\frac{6}{17}$ + $\frac{3}{17}$ = $\frac{9}{17}$ ❷

b In a survey 29 students were asked if they like celery or rhubarb. 12 said they like celery, 13 said they like rhubarb and 11 said they like neither celery nor rhubarb. The Venn diagram shows this information. One of these students is picked at random. Find the probability that this student likes
  i celery
  ii rhubarb
  iii celery and rhubarb
  iv celery or rhubarb.

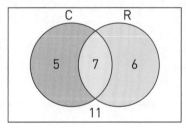

Answers

b i P(C) = $\frac{\text{total number of successful outcomes}}{\text{total number of possible outcomes}}$ = $\frac{12}{29}$ ❶

  ii P(R) = $\frac{\text{total number of successful outcomes}}{\text{total number of possible outcomes}}$ = $\frac{13}{29}$ ❶

  iii 7 students like celery and rhubarb.

  So P(C and R) = $\frac{\text{total number of successful outcomes}}{\text{total number of possible outcomes}}$ = $\frac{7}{29}$ ❶

  iv Liking celery and liking rhubarb are not mutually exclusive, 7 students like both, so P(C or R) = P(C) + P(R) − P(C and R);

  P(C or R) = $\frac{12}{29}$ + $\frac{13}{29}$ − $\frac{7}{29}$ = $\frac{18}{29}$

Exam-style questions

1 The Venn diagram shows information about the numbers and colours of beads in a bag.

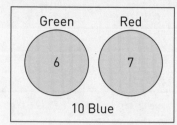

A bead is taken at random from the bag. Find the probability that the bead will be
a   green
b   green or blue
c   green and red. **[4]**

2 67 people go to a concert. 35 of these people buy a programme, 27 buy an ice cream and 18 buy neither a programme nor an ice cream. Some people buy both.
a   Draw a Venn diagram to show this information. **[3]**
b   One of these people is picked at random. Find the probability that this person buys
    i   only a programme
    ii   a programme or an ice cream. **[3]**

3 A and B are two independent events:
P(A) = 0.8, P(B) = 0.5
a   Find P(A and B) **[2]**
b   Find P(A or B) **[2]**

CHECKED ANSWERS

Statistics and probability: exam-style questions

1 The stem and leaf diagram gives information about the speeds, in miles per hour, of 25 cars on a road.

2	5 7 9 9 9 9
3	0 0 0 0 0 0 2 3 3 4 4 5 5 5 7
4	1 1 5
5	2

Key: 2|5 represents 25 miles per hour

  a Find
    i the median speed   ii the range.   **[3]**
  b Draw a frequency diagram for this information. Use the groups $20 \leqslant s < 30, 30 \leqslant s < 40$ and so on. **[3]**
  c What do you think is the speed limit for this road? Give a reason for your answer.   **[1]**

2 John recorded the times taken, in minutes, for each of eight students to complete a 250-piece jigsaw puzzle and a 500-piece jigsaw puzzle. His results are given in the table.

250-piece jigsaw (minutes)	35	41	70	71	62	74	45	51
500-piece jigsaw (minutes)	68	70	70	90	86	99	75	78

  a Draw a scatter diagram for this information.   **[3]**
  b One of the data points may be an outlier. Which data point? Give a reason for your answer.   **[1]**
  c Describe and interpret the correlation.   **[2]**
  Kyle is another student. It takes him 57 minutes to do the 250-piece jigsaw.
  d i Find an estimate for how long it takes him to do the 500-piece jigsaw.
    ii Comment on the reliability of your estimate.   **[3]**

3 An insurance company received a total of 3467 claims last year. Of these 2125 were for household damage. This year the insurance company expects to receive a total of 5000 claims.
Estimate the number of claims for household damage this year.   **[2]**

4 Cheri spins a fair 5-sided spinner, numbered 1, 2, 3, 4 and 5, and rolls an ordinary dice.
What is the probability that Cheri will get
  a a 3 on the spinner and a 3 on the dice   **[2]**
  b a 3 on the spinner or a 3 on the dice?   **[2]**

5 Bag A contains 3 red counters and 2 green counters. Bag B contains 4 red counters and 5 green counters. Bag C contains 1 red counter and 6 green counters. Hamish is going to take at random a counter from bag A. If he takes a red counter he will take a counter at random from bag B. If he takes a green counter he will take a counter at random from bag C.
Work out the probability that both counters will be the same colour.   **[4]**

6 Nima rolls 5 ordinary dice. Work out the probability that he will get exactly three 6s.   **[3]**

7 24 people gave presents on Mother's day. 7 people gave only flowers. 5 people gave only chocolates, x people gave both flowers and chocolates, and 9 people gave neither flowers nor chocolates.
  a Draw a Venn diagram to show this information.   **[3]**
  b Work out the value of x.   **[2]**
  c One of these people is picked at random. Find the probability that this person gave
    i both flowers and chocolates
    ii flowers or chocolates or both.   **[3]**

The language used in mathematics examinations

- **You must show your working...** you will lose marks if working is not shown.

- **Estimate...** often means round numbers to 1 s.f.

- **Calculate...** some working out is needed; so show it!

- **Work out/find...** a written or mental calculation is needed.

- **Write down...** written working out is not usually required.

- **Give an exact value of...** no rounding or approximations:
  - on a calculator paper, write down all the numbers on your calculator.
  - on a non-calculator paper, give your answer in terms of π.

- **Give your answer to an appropriate degree of accuracy...** if the numbers in the question are given to 2 d.p. give your answer to 2 d.p.

- **Give your answer in its simplest form...** usually cancelling of a fraction or a ratio is required.

- **Simplify...** collect like terms together in an algebraic expression.

- **Solve...** usually means find the value of x in an equation.

- **Expand...** multiply out brackets.

- **Construct, using ruler and compasses...** the ruler is to be used as a straight edge and compasses must be used to draw arcs. You **must** show all your construction lines.

- **Measure...** use a ruler or a protractor to accurately measure lengths or angles.

- **Draw an accurate diagram...** use a ruler and protractor – lengths must be exact, angles must be accurate.

- **Make y the subject of the formula...** rearrange the formula to get y on its own on one side e.g. $y = \frac{2x - 3}{4}$

- **Sketch...** an accurate drawing is not required – freehand drawing will be accepted.

- **Diagram NOT accurately drawn...** don't measure angles or sides – you must calculate them if you are asked for them.

- **Give reasons for your answer... OR explain why...** worded explanations are required referring to the theory used.

- **Use your/the graph...** read the values from your graph and use them.

- **Describe fully...** usually transformations:
  - Translation
  - Reflection in a line
  - Rotation through an angle about a point
  - Enlargement by a scale factor about a point

- **Give a reason for your answer...** usually in angle questions, a written reason is required e.g. 'angles in a triangle add up to 180°' or 'corresponding angles', etc.

- **You must explain your answer...** a worded explanation is required along with the answer.

- **Show how you got your answer...** show all your working. Words may also be needed.

- **Describe...** answer the question using words.

- **Write down any assumption you make...** describe any things you have assumed are true when giving your answer.

- **Show...** usually requires you to use algebra or reasons to show something is true.

Exam technique and formulae that will be given

- Be prepared and know what to expect.

- Don't just learn key points.

- Work through past papers. Start from the back and work towards the easier questions. Your teacher will be able to help you.

- Practice is the key, it won't just happen.

- Read the question thoroughly.

- Cross out answers if you change them, only give **one** answer.

- Underline the key facts in the question.

- Estimate the answer.

- Is the answer right/realistic?

- Have the right equipment.
  - Calculator
  - Pens
  - Pencils
  - Ruler, compass, protractor
  - Eraser
  - Tracing paper
  - Spares

- Never give two different answers to a question.

- Never just give just an answer if there is more than 1 mark.

- Never measure diagrams; most diagrams are not drawn accurately.

- Never just give the rounded answer; always show the full answer in the working space.

- Read each question carefully.

- Show stages in your working.

- Check your answer has the units.

- Work steadily through the paper.

- Skip questions you cannot do and then go back to them if time allows.

- Use marks as a guide for time: 1 mark = 1 min

- Present clear answers at the bottom of the space provided.

● Go back to questions you did not do.

● Read the information below the diagram – this is accurate.

● Use mnemonics to help remember formula you will need, for example:
  ○ SOH   sin = opposite/hypotenuse
  ○ CAH   cos = adjacent/hypotenuse
  ○ TOA   tan = opposite/adjacent
  ○ or 'silly old hens cackle and hale, till old age'.
  ○ For the order of operations, BIDMAS: Brackets, Indices, Division, Multiply, Add, Subtract
  ○ Formula triangles for the relationship between three parameters e.g. speed, distance and time

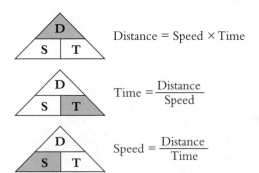 Distance = Speed × Time

Time $= \dfrac{\text{Distance}}{\text{Speed}}$

Speed $= \dfrac{\text{Distance}}{\text{Time}}$

● The following formulae will be provided for students within the relevant examination questions. All other formulae and rules **must** be learnt.
Where r is the radius of the sphere or cone, l is the slant height of a cone and h is the perpendicular height of a cone:

  ○ Curved surface area of a cone = $\pi r l$
  ○ Volume of a cone = $\frac{1}{3}\pi r^2 h$
  ○ Surface area of a sphere = $4\pi r^2$
  ○ Volume of a sphere = $\frac{4}{3}\pi r^3$

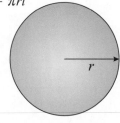 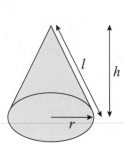

Common areas where students make mistakes

Here are some topics that students frequently make errors in during their exam.

Number

> **Rules**
>
> ❶ A factor is a number that divides into another number, e.g. 2 is a factor of 6.
> ❷ A multiple is a member of the multiplication table of that number, e.g. 6 is a multiple of 2.
> ❸ A prime number is one that can only be divided by 1 and itself, e.g. 2, 3, 5, 7, 11 ...

	Question	Working	Answer
Highest Common Factor (HCF)	Find the HCF of 24 and 36.	Use factor trees to find all the factors of 24 and 36: $24 = 2 \times 2 \times 2 \times 3$ $36 = 2 \times 2 \times 3 \times 3$ The common factors are: $2 \times 2 \times 3 = 12$	12
Lowest Common Multiple (LCM)	Find the LCM of 9 and 12.	List the multiples of 9 and 12: 9, 18, 27, 36, 45 12, 24, 36, 48	36

	Question	Working	Answer
Adding	$\frac{2}{3} + \frac{1}{4}$	Write equivalent fractions: $\frac{2}{3} = \frac{4}{6} = \frac{6}{9} = \frac{8}{12}$ and $\frac{1}{4} = \frac{2}{8} = \frac{3}{12}$ 12 is the LCM of 3 and 4 so write the fractions in 12ths: $\frac{8}{12} + \frac{3}{12} = \frac{8+3}{12} = \frac{11}{12}$	$\frac{11}{12}$
Subtracting	$\frac{2}{3} - \frac{1}{4}$	You use the same method as adding but just take away, so we get: $\frac{8}{12} - \frac{3}{12} = \frac{8-3}{12} = \frac{5}{12}$	$\frac{5}{12}$
Multiplying	$\frac{2}{5} \times \frac{3}{8}$	Multiply the tops together and then the bottoms of the fractions: $\frac{2 \times 3}{5 \times 8} = \frac{6}{40}$ then cancel by 2	$\frac{3}{20}$
Dividing	$\frac{5}{12} \div \frac{2}{3}$	Write the first fraction down and turn the second fraction upside down and multiply: $\frac{5}{12} \times \frac{3}{2} = \frac{15}{24}$ then cancel by 3	$\frac{5}{8}$

	Question	Working	Answer
Changing a fraction to a decimal	Write $\frac{3}{8}$ as a decimal.	Divide the top number by the bottom number so divide 3 by 8: $$\begin{array}{r} 0.375 \\ 8\overline{\smash{)}3.^30^60^40} \end{array}$$	0.375

	Question	Working	Answer
Finding a fraction of an amount	Find $\frac{3}{5}$ of £4.80.	This can be written as $\frac{3}{5} \times £4.80$ There is a simple rule for this calculation, which is 'Divide by the bottom and Times by the top' You can sing it to the 'Wheels on the bus' song to help you remember it. £4.80 ÷ 5 = 0.96 then 0.96 × 3 = £2.88	£2.88
Finding a percentage of an amount	Work out 60% of £4.80.	This can be written as $\frac{60}{100} \times £4.80$. You can use the same rule so you divide by 100 and times by 60: £4.80 ÷ 100 × 60 = £2.88	£2.88

	Question	Working	Answer
Estimating	Estimate $\frac{76.15 \times 0.49}{19.04}$	Write each number to one significant figure so that: 76.15 becomes 80 0.49 becomes 0.5 19.04 becomes 20 Remember that the size of the estimate needs to be similar to the original number. So 80 × 0.5 = 40 and 40 ÷ 20 = 2	2

	Question	Working	Answer
Using a calculator	Work out $\frac{76.15 + 5.62^2}{19.04}$	You either need to enter the whole calculation into your calculator using the fraction button or work out the top first then divide the answer by the bottom. $76.15 + 5.62^2 = 107.7344$ 107.73 ÷ 19.04 = 5.658 319 327	5.658 319 327

Algebra

Rules

$2y + y = 3y$; $2y - y = y$; $2y \times y = 2y^2$; $2y \div y = 2$

$y^m \times y^n = y^{m+n}$ $y^m \div y^n = y^{m-n}$ $(y^m)^n = y^{mn}$

	Question	Working	Answer
Collecting like terms	Simplify		
	a $2ab + 3ab - ab$	$= 2ab + 3ab - 1ab$	$4ab$
	b $3y^2 - y^2$	$= 3y^2 - 1y^2$	$2y^2$

	Question	Working	Answer
Index laws	Simplify		
	a $x^4 \times x^5$	$= x^{4+5}$	x^9
	b $\frac{a^7}{a^3}$	$= \frac{a^7}{a^3} = a^7 \div a^3 = a^{7-3}$	a^4
	c $(y^2)^3$	$= y^{2 \times 3}$	y^6
	d $7f^4g^3 \times 2f^3g$	$= 7 \times 2 \times f^{4+3} \times g^{3+1}$	$14f^7g^4$

	Question	Working	Answer
Multiplying out the brackets	Expand		
	a $3(4p + 5)$	$= 3 \times 4p + 3 \times 5$	$12p + 15$
	b $7p - 4(p - q)$	$= 7p - 4 \times p - 4 \times -q = 7p - 4p + 4q$	$3p + 4q$
	c $(y + 3)(y - 4)$	$= y \times y + y \times -4 + 3 \times y + 3 \times -4$	
		$= y^2 - 4y + 3y - 12$	$y^2 - y - 12$

	Question	Working	Answer
Factorising expressions	Factorise completely		
	a $5ab + 10bc$	$= 5 \times a \times b + 2 \times 5 \times b \times c$	$5b(a + 2c)$
	b $12e^2f - 9ef^2$	$= 3 \times 4 \times e \times e \times f - 3 \times 3 \times e \times f \times f$	$3ef(4e - 3f)$
	c $x^2 + 7x + 12$	$= x^2 + (3 + 4)x + 3 \times 4$	$(x + 3)(x + 4)$

	Question	Working	Answer
Solving equations	Solve		
	a $3t - 2 = 4$	$3t = 4 + 2$ so $3t = 6$	$t = 2$
	b $3f + 4 = 5f - 3$	$4 + 3 = 5f - 3f$ so $7 = 2f$ or $2f = 7$	$f = 3.5$
	c $5(x + 2) = 3$	$5x + 10 = 3$ so $5x = 3 - 10$ or $5x = -7$	$x = -1.4$
	d $y^2 - 3y - 10 = 0$	$(y + 2)(y - 5) = 0$ so $y + 2 = 0$ or $y - 5 = 0$	$y = -2$ or $y = 5$

Geometry and measure

Rules

The **perimeter** of a shape is the distance around its edge. You **add** all the side lengths together.

The **area** of a shape is the amount of flat surface it has. You **multiply** two lengths.

The **volume** of a shape is the amount of space it has. You **multiply** three lengths.

Alternate angles are in the shape of a letter **Z**.

Corresponding angles are in the shape of a letter **F**.

Allied angles or co-interior angles are in the shape of a letter **C**.

	Question	Working	Answer
Perimeter of a shape	Find the perimeter of this shape. 3 cm ☐ 5 cm	For a rectangle you need to add the lengths of the four sides. 3 + 5 + 3 + 5 = 16	 16 cm

	Question	Working	Answer
Area of a shape	Find the area of this shape. 3 cm ◺ 6 cm	For this right-angled triangle you need to use the formula: Area = $\frac{1}{2}$ base × vertical height So the area = $\frac{1}{2} \times 6 \times 3 = 9$ You have multiplied two lengths.	 9 cm²

	Question	Working	Answer
Volume of a solid	Find the volume of this shape with radius 5 cm and height 12 cm in terms of π.	For this cylinder you need to use the formula: Volume = $\pi \times r^2 \times h$ So volume is $\pi \times 5 \times 5 \times 12 = 300\pi$ You have multiplied three lengths.	 300π cm³

	Question	Working and answer
Angles between parallel lines	Find the missing angles in this diagram. Give reasons for your answer. 50° a b c	$a = 50°$ (Alternate angles are equal) $b = 130°$ (Allied angles add to 180° (supplementary)) $c = 50°$ (Corresponding angles are equal)

	Question	Working and answer
Finding missing angles and giving reasons	*ABC* is an isosceles triangle. *BCD* is a straight line. Find, giving reasons, angle *ACD*. A 50° D C B	Angle *ABC* = (180 – 50) ÷ 2 = 65° (The three angles of a triangle add to 180°) Angle *ACB* = Angle *ABC* = 65° (Base angles of an isosceles triangle are equal) Angle *ACD* = 180 – 65 = 115° (Sum of the angles on a straight line = 180°)

Statistics and probability

	Question	Working	Answer
Mean from a grouped frequency table	Work out an estimate of the mean age from this frequency table. 	Age	f
---	---
$0 < a \leq 10$	4
$10 < a \leq 20$	6
$20 < a \leq 30$	12
$30 < a \leq 40$	5
$40 < a \leq 50$	3		Multiply the mid value of the age groups by the frequency. $5 \times 4 = 20$ $15 \times 6 = 90$ $25 \times 12 = 300$ $35 \times 5 = 175$ $45 \times 3 = 135$ Divide the **total** of age × frequency by the **total frequency**: $720 \div 30$ Note: Don't forget to divide by the total frequency and not the number of groups (5).	24

	Question	Working	Answer
Pie chart	Draw a pie chart from this information. 	Favourite colour	f
---	---
Red	7
Blue	4
Green	2
Yellow	3
Black	4		As pie charts are based on a circle then we need to divide the number of degrees in a whole turn (360°) by the total frequency which is 20. So $360° \div 20 = 18°$ The angle for each colour is then calculated by multiplying its frequency by 18°.	Red = $7 \times 18° = 126°$ Blue = $4 \times 18° = 72°$ Green = $2 \times 18° = 36°$ Yellow = $3 \times 18° = 54°$ Black = $4 \times 18° = 72°$ Then draw the circular pie chart.

Common areas where students make mistakes 119

One week to go

You need to know these formulae and essential techniques.

Number

Topic	Formula		When to use it
Negative numbers	+ + = +	− − = +	Two signs next to each other
	+ − = −	− + = −	
	+ × + = +	− × − = +	Multiplying integers
	+ × − = −	− × + = −	
	+ ÷ + = +	− ÷ − = +	Dividing integers
	+ ÷ − = −	− ÷ + = −	
Order of operations	BIDMAS		If you have to carry out a calculation. You use the order Brackets, Indices, Division, Multiplication, Addition and Subtraction.
Percentages	20% of $50 = \frac{20}{100} \times 50$		To find the percentage of an amount e.g. 20% of 50.
Simple interest	SI for 5 years at 3% on £150 $\frac{3}{100} \times 150 \times 5$		To find the **simple interest** you find the interest for one year and multiply by the number of years.
Compound interest	CI for 2 years at 3% on £150 Year 1 $\frac{3}{100} \times 150 = £4.50$ Year 2 $\frac{3}{100} \times (150 + 4.50)$		For **compound interest** you find the percentage interest for one year, add it to the initial amount and find the interest on the total and so on. You can also do this using geometric progressions and write £150 × (1.03)² =
Standard form	$2.5 \times 10^3 = 2500$ $2.5 \times 10^{-3} = 0.0025$		A number in standard form is (a number between 1 and 10) × (a power of 10)
Approximating	Decimal places		You round to a number of decimal places by looking at the next decimal place and rounding up or down.
	Significant figures		The first non-zero digit is always the first significant figure and you count the number of significant figures then look at the next figure and round up or down. You should always keep the idea of the size of the number.

Algebra

Topic	Formula	When to use it
Rules of indices	$y^m \times y^n = y^{m+n}$	When you multiply you add the indices or powers.
	$y^m \div y^n = y^{m-n}$	When you divide you subtract the indices or powers.
	$(y^m)^n = y^{mn}$	When you raise a power to a power you multiply the indices or powers.
Straight line graph	$y = mx + c$	m is the gradient and $(0, c)$ the intercept on the y-axis.

Geometry and measure

Topic	Formula	When to use it
Parallel sides		Parallel lines are shown with arrows.
Equal sides		Equal lines are shown with short lines.
Perimeter	Add lengths of all sides.	To find the perimeter of any 2D shape
Areas of 2D shapes	Area = $l \times w$	Area of a rectangle is length × width
	Area = $\frac{1}{2}b \times h$	Area of a triangle is $\frac{1}{2}$ base × vertical height
	Area = $b \times h$	Area of a parallelogram is base × vertical height
	Area = $\frac{1}{2}(a + b) \times h$	Area of a trapezium is $\frac{1}{2}$ the sum of the parallel sides × the vertical height
Circumference and area of a circle	$C = \pi \times D$ or $C = \pi \times 2r$	Circumference or the perimeter of a circle is: pi × diameter **or** pi × double the radius
	$A = \pi \times r^2$	Area of a circle is pi × radius squared

Volumes of 3D shapes	$V = l \times w \times h$	Volume of a cuboid is:
		Length × width × height
	$V = \pi r^2 h$	Volume of a cylinder is:
		Area of circular end × height
Pythagoras' theorem	$h = \sqrt{a^2 + b^2}$ $a = \sqrt{h^2 - b^2}$ $b = \sqrt{h^2 - a^2}$	The hypotenuse of a right-angled triangle can be found by finding the square root of the sum of the squares of the two shorter sides. A shorter side of a right-angled triangle can be found by finding the square root of the difference between the hypotenuse squared and the other shorter side squared.
Trigonometry	$sin = \frac{o}{h}$ $cos = \frac{a}{h}$ $tan = \frac{o}{a}$	You can find a missing side or a missing angle by selecting and using one of these formulae. You use the trigonometry ratio that has two given pieces of information and the one you have to find.

Statistics and probability

Topic	Formula	When to use it
Probability	$\mathbf{P}(A \text{ and } B) = \mathbf{P}(A) \times \mathbf{P}(B)$	You use this when you have two independent events.
	$\mathbf{P}(A \text{ or } B) = \mathbf{P}(A) + \mathbf{P}(B)$	You use this when you have mutually exclusive events.
	$\mathbf{P}(A \text{ or } B) = \mathbf{P}(A) + \mathbf{P}(B)$ $\qquad\qquad - \mathbf{P}(A) \times \mathbf{P}(B)$	You use this when you do not have mutually exclusive events.

Answers

Number

Pre-revision check (page 1)

1 a 8.5   b 18   c 1.4

2 a 25.392   b 56.7

3 a 26.1   b 26.38

4 a 0.018   b 124.5   c 254 900   d 48.7

5 a 5.72×10^{-3} b 31 840

6 a 5357.142... or 5.357... $\times 10^3$

   b 2302 or 2.302... $\times 10^3$

7 a 16.4   b 16.35   c 16.355

8 a 0.002   b 0.0015   c 0.001 55

9 a 3000   b 0.003

10 lower bound = 8.365 upper bound = 8.375

11 a $\frac{5}{18}$ b $\frac{3}{55}$ c 9   d $\frac{1}{2}$

12 a $\frac{11}{60}$ b $3\frac{5}{12}$ c $18\frac{4}{15}$ d 10   e $1\frac{1}{5}$

13 a i 55% ii 190%   b i $\frac{3}{50}$ ii 0.06

14 a £13   b 374 m   15 a 8%   b 25%

16 £112 000   17 £22 861.89

18 a 105, 175   b $\frac{5}{9}$

19 1976 g or 1.976 kg

20 A = inverse, B = direct, C = inverse

21 $T = \frac{35}{x}$

22 a 3^5 b 3^5 c 3^{18}

23 a 4   b 10 000

24 $2 \times 2 \times 3 \times 3 \times 5 \times 7$

BIDMAS (page 3)

1 a 4   b $3 + (9 - 5) \times 2 = 11$

2 $7 - 10 \div (3 + 2) = 5$ 3 .9435...

Multiplying decimals (page 4)

1 614.6

2 Shop A (£64.32) is cheaper than Shop B (£64.80)

3 £10.48

Dividing decimals (page 5)

1 £7.92   2 6 (6.65)   3 £253.60

Using the number system effectively (page 6)

1 a 0.539   b 4580

2 a 4165   b 11.9   c 0.833

Understanding standard form (page 7)

1 a 7.2×10^{-2} b 2.389×10^5

2 a 9 140 000   b 0.000 518   3 17×10^{-2}

Calculating with standard form (page 8)

1 a 4.5188×10^3 b $3.994... \times 10^9$

2 0.29 nanometre   3 6.324×10^4

Rounding to decimal places, significance and approximating (page 9)

1 $11.44 \, \text{cm}^2$ 2 11.5 cm   3 2000

Limits of accuracy (page 10)

1 a 2.25 m and 1.15 m   b 2.35 m and 1.25 m

2 2495 m or 2.495 km

3 No. The average speed is between $61\frac{2}{3}$ and 65 mph

Multiplying and dividing fractions (page 11)

1 a $\frac{1}{48}$ b $\frac{20}{9}$ 2 a $\frac{1}{6}$ b $\frac{2}{15}$

Adding and subtracting fractions and working with mixed numbers (page 12)

1 a $\frac{23}{24}$ b $2\frac{5}{6}$

2 a $\frac{5}{8}$ b $\frac{9}{40}$ 3 $11\frac{1}{3} \, \text{m}^2$

Converting fractions and decimals to and from percentages (page 13)

1 20%   0.202   0.21 $\frac{2}{9}$ $\frac{1}{4}$

2 0.031 818 18...   3   21.25%

Applying percentage increases and decreases to amounts (page 14)

1 12.75 cm

2 £405 in the auction, so could have £5 more

3 108 before and 104 after, so less

Finding the percentage change from one amount to another (page 15)

1 2.5%   2 3.75% loss

3 Nazia (15%) more than Debra (14.5%)

Reverse percentages (page 16)

1 £320   2 No, he had 5019 in 2014

3 Better off by £234.89

Repeated percentage increase/decrease (page 17)

1 £4589.95(6)   2 No   3 3 years

Mixed exam-style questions (page 18)

1 $5 \times (2 + 3) - 7 = 18.$ $5 \times 2 + (3 - 7) = 6$

2 No, Naomi = £446.95 and Izmail = £441

3 a tube = 1.2 p per sweet, box = 1.25 p per sweet

   b 1 box and 2 tubes

4 a 1.6107   b 158.34

5 255×10^{-1} 0.0026×10^5 $25 \div 10^{-2}$

   2.56×10^3 26×10^2

6 a $0.5 \times 7.6 \times 4.0 = 15.2\,\text{cm}^2$

  b less since both dimensions are less

7 Noreen is right (area = 46.2)

8 £7200

9 a 30.2 **b** 7.8×10^8

10 Yes, since $30.5 \times 18.5 = 564.25\,\text{cm}^2$

Sharing in a given ratio (page 19)

1 £60, £48, £24 **2** 6384 **3** Small packet

Working with proportional quantities (page 20)

1 £9.75 **2** £1.35 **3** 88

The constant of proportionality (page 21)

1 a 4.00, 8.10, 8.00 **b** E = 1.35P

  c the exchange rate

2 87.5

Working with inversely proportional quantities (page 22)

1 a inverse, since $8 \times 25 = 10 \times 20 = 200$

  b 50 days

2 $x = 25$, $y = 12$ (not 120) **3** 10

Index notation and rules of indices (page 23)

1 a 10^4 **b** 32768 **2** 2^{15}

3 $10^4 \times 10^5 = 10^9$, $10 \times 10^2 = 10^3$, $\frac{10^{20}}{10^2} = 10^{18}$,
$10^{10} = 10\,000\,000\,000$

Prime factorisation (page 24)

1 a $2 \times 2 \times 2 \times 2 \times 2 \times 3$

  b i 24 **ii** 480

2 Saturday 8 am

Mixed exam-style questions (page 25)

1 a $\frac{5}{8}$ **b** $\frac{1}{4}$

2 $3\frac{13}{63}$ hours

3 Rachel

4 a 1363 **b** 23.5% **5** $\frac{6}{35}$

6 a Bill, since Bill = $1.25\,\text{m}^3$ Sandra = $1.23\,\text{m}^3$

  b Less needed, since $\frac{2}{19} < \frac{1}{8}$

7 Medium

8 £840

9 a $y = kx$ and $x = cz$, so $y = kcx = \text{constant} \times z$

  b 50

10 a s is inversely proportional to **b** $3\frac{1}{3}$

11 −2.5 **12** 1254

Algebra

Pre-revision check (page 27)

1 8

2 a $a = 2$ **b** $b = 15$ **c** $c = \frac{2}{5}$ **d** $e = -6$

3 a i $10a + 15$ **ii** $3h^2 - 6h$ **iii** $12x^2 - 6xy$

  b i $6(y + 2)$ **ii** $3p(2p - 3)$

  iii $5e(e + 2f)$ **iv** $4xy(2x - 3y)$

4 a $x = 3$ **b** $p = -0.75$ **c** $y = -1\frac{1}{11}$

5 a $g = 3$ **b** $h = -\frac{2}{7}$ **c** $k = -7$

6 a i a^{10} **ii** x^3 **iii** $\frac{3f^2}{2e^3}$ or $\frac{3}{2}f^2e^{-3}$

  b i $t^2 + 7t + 10$ **ii** $v^2 - 2v - 35$

  iii $y^2 - 11y + 30$

7 a 100 **b** $a = \frac{2(S - ut)}{t^2}$

8 $n - 1 + n + n - 1 = 3n$. This is a multiple of 3 since 3 is always a factor.

9 a $6n - 2$ **b** 298

  c If $6n - 2 = 900$ then $6n = 902$ and $n = 150.3$. The term numbers must be whole numbers so 900 is not a member of the sequence.

10 a −1, 5, 15, 29, 47, ...

  b $n^2 + 2n$ or $n(n + 2)$

11 30 **12 a** 3 **b** 98415

13 a by inspection **b** $x = 2.5$

14 08 00 and 13:00 **15** $y = 3x - 2$

16 a by inspection **b** $x = 3.6$ or −0.6

17 $y = -\frac{1}{2}x + \frac{3}{2}$

18 a by inspection **b** $x = 1$ and $x = 3$ **c** $x = 2$

19 a by inspection **b** $x = -2.3$ or $x = 0$ or $x = 1.3$

20 a $-3 \leqslant x < 4$

  b i $x < 2$ **ii** $t > 1.2$ **iii** $y \leqslant 4.5$

21 $x = 2$, $y = -1$ **22** $x = \frac{1}{2}$, $y = 2$

23 a i $x^2 - x - 20$ **ii** $y^2 - 64$ **iii** $36 - a^2$

  b i $(x + 3)(x + 4)$ **ii** $(e - 5)(e + 2)$

  iii $(b + 5)(b - 5)$

24 a $x = 2$ or $x = 3$ **b** $x = 5$ or $x = -3$

  c $x = 7$ or $x = -7$

Working with formulae (page 29)

1 a 10 **b** 90

2 a 2 hours or 120 minutes **b** 4.5 kg

Setting up and solving simple equations (page 30)

1 a $a = 10$ **b** $b = 15$ **c** $c = -\frac{2}{3}$

  d $d = 10$ **e** $e = 1.5$ **2** $76\,\text{cm}^2$

Using brackets (page 31)

1 Amy is 8, Beth is 11 and Cath is 22 **2** 36 cm

Solving equations with the unknown on both sides (page 32)

1 $104\,\text{cm}^2$

2 $2x + 30 = 5x - 15$; $45 = 3x$; $x = 15$
Substituting $x = 15$ into each expression gives 60° for each angle. Therefore triangle ABC is equilateral.

Solving equations with brackets (page 33)

1 $n = 6$ **2** $2250\,cm^2$

Simplifying harder expressions and expanding two brackets (page 34)

1 a $\dfrac{3y^6}{4}$ **b** $\dfrac{5a^3b^2}{4}$

2 $(2a + 5)(a + 3) - a^2 = 2a^2 + 6a + 5a + 15 - a^2 = a^2 + 11a + 15$

Using complex formulae and changing the subject of a formula (page 35)

1 -540 **2** $t = \sqrt{\dfrac{y - 3s}{5a}}$

Identities (page 36)

1 $x^2 - 7x + 12 = (x - 3)(x - 4)$
so $p = -3$ and $q = -4$ or vice versa

2 $(2n + 1)(2m + 1)$ $2n + 1$ is one consecutive number and $2m + 1$ is another

$4mn + 2n + 2m + 1$
$= 2(2mn + n + m) + 1$
$= 2p + 1$ $2 \times$ another number p plus 1

Linear sequences (page 37)

1 a 27 **b** $4n + 3$
  c Yes. $4n + 3 = 163$ so $4n = 160$ and $n = 40$

2 n^{th} term is $59 - 4n$ so $59 - 4n < 0$ so $59 < 4n$ therefore $n > 14.75$ which makes $n = 15$

Special sequences (page 38)

1 a $n^2 + 1$ **b** 401   **2** $(n + 1)(n + 2)$

Quadratic sequences (page 39)

1 14 and 34   **2** $2n^2 + 5$

Geometric progressions (page 40)

1 a 2.5 **b** 1171.875 **2** £5796.37

Mixed exam-style questions (page 41)

1 a 37°C **b** −40°C   **2** 10 20 am

3 $\dfrac{40x + 60}{4} = 10x + 15$, $\dfrac{40x + 60}{5} = 8x + 12$, $10x + 15 - (8x + 12) = 2x + 3$

4 17

5 Area of one triangle is $\frac{1}{2}(x + 2)(5x - 3)$
$= \frac{1}{2}(5x^2 + 7x - 6)$
Area of 4 triangles is $10x^2 + 14x - 12$
Length of large square is $x + 2 + 5x - 3 = 6x - 1$
Area of large square is $(6x - 1)^2 = 36x^2 - 12x + 1$
Red square area is $36x^2 - 12x + 1 - (10x^2 + 14x - 12) = 26x^2 - 26x + 13 = 13(2x^2 - 2x + 1)$
  a $n + n + 1 + n + 2 + 10 + n + 1 + 20 + n + 1 = 5n + 35 = 5(n + 7)$
  b If $5n + 35 = 130$; then $n = 19$. n cannot equal 19 because it will overlap the grid.

7 a Week 7: 800, Week 5: 1600, Week 3: 3200, Week 1: 6400
  b $800 \times \left(\dfrac{1}{\sqrt{2}}\right)^3 = 282$ to 283

Plotting graphs of linear functions (page 42)

1 a Accurate graph of $y = 20x + 40$
  b 6 days

2 a

x	−3	−2	−1	0	1	2	3
y	−7	−5	−3	−1	1	3	5

  b Accurate graph of $y = 2x - 1$ **c** $x = 2.5$

Real-life graphs (page 44)

a 08 00   **b** 15 minutes   **c** 30 minutes
d 10 15   **e** 9 miles   **f** 1 hour
g 45 minutes   **h** 12 miles per hour

The equation of a straight line (page 45)

1 $y = 2x - 1$

2 P, S and T are parallel to each other and so are Q and R

Plotting quadratic and cubic graphs (page 46)

1 a by inspection   **b** $x = 1$ or $x = 3$

2 by inspection

Finding equations of straight lines (page 47)

1 $y = 3x + 3$ **2** $y = -2x + 1$

Quadratic functions (page 48)

1 a accurate graph   **b** $y = x^2 - 2x - 8$
2 a accurate graph
  b Roots are +3 and −3 **c** Maximum point is $(0, 9)$

Polynomial and reciprocal functions (page 49)

1 a accurate graph
  b All three meet at $(0, 0)$, $(1, 1)$ and $y = x$ and $y = x^3$ also meet at $(-1, -1)$

2 Fuel consumption approaches 60

Linear inequalities (page 50)

1 a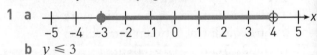
  b $y \leqslant 3$

2 A number less than 10

Solving simultaneous equations by elimination and substitution (page 51)

1 $a = 2$ and $b = 3$

2 12 ordinary coaches and 3 superior coaches

Using graphs to solve simultaneous equations (page 52)

1 $x = -1$ and $y = -1$

2 Peach up to 40 Mbytes. At 40 Mbytes both companies. After 40 Mbytes M−mobile.

Factorising quadratics of the form $x^2 + bx + c$ (page 53)

1 $x^2 + 6x + 8 = (x + 2)(x + 4)$
2 $x^2 - 2x - 8 = (x + 2)(x - 4)$
3 $x^2 + 2x - 8 = (x - 2)(x + 4)$
4 $x^2 - 6x + 8 = (x - 2)(x - 4)$
5 $x^2 - 16 = (x + 4)(x - 4)$

Solve equations by factorising (page 54)

1 a $x = -6$ or $x = 2$ b $x = 0$ or $x = 5$
   c $x = 9$ or $x = -2$ d $x = +5$ or $x = -5$
2 Ben could use 2 or -12

Mixed exam-style questions (page 55)

1 a £80   b £15
   c Up to 2 days cheaper with Car Co, 3 days or more is cheaper with Cars 4 U
2 Accurate graph of line $y = 2x + 1$
3 a $2y = 3x + 4$ b $y + 4x = -2$
4 a $y = -1$ b $x = 3.3$ $y = 0.7$; $x = -0.3$ $y = 4.3$
5 a $y = 2x - 7$

b Substituting in the values of x and y from $(3, -1)$ gives $y = -1$ and $2 \times 3 - 7 = 6 - 7$ which also gives -1
Therefore the point $(3, -1)$ lies on the line l.
6 a accurate graph
   b $y = (x - 2)^2$ or $y = x^2 - 4x + 4$
7 a Accurate graph
   b About 4.5 pence per mile
8 Cathy is 24
9 $a = 7$ and $b = 1$;   Triangle's area is $24\,\text{cm}^2$; Rectangle's area is $75\,\text{cm}^2$
10 $(1, 4)$; $(4, \frac{1}{2})$; and $(-3, -3)$
11 $(x - 8)$ is the width and $(x - 4)$ is the length
12 $30\,\text{cm}$

Geometry and Measures

Pre-revision check (page 57)

1 a by inspection   b $55°$
2 a $17\,\text{m}$ b $14\,\text{cm}$ 3 $86.4\,\text{m}$ 4 $14.98\,\text{g}$
5 a Trapezium   b Square, Rhombus
   c Rectangle, Parallelogram, Rhombus
6 $a = 67°$ $b = 67°$
7 exterior angle = $30°$, interior angle = $150°$
8 A and C, SAS
9 All equilateral triangles have angles of $60°$, therefore all equilateral triangles are similar. Equilateral triangles can have different length sides, therefore not all equilateral triangles are congruent.
10 area = $78.54\,\text{cm}^2$, circumference = $31.42\,\text{cm}$
11 $8.1\,\text{cm}$ 1 d.p.   12 a $14.7\,\text{cm}$ b $51.3\,\text{cm}^2$
13 Accurate drawing of triangle XYZ, XZ = $8\,\text{cm}$, YX = $6.5\,\text{cm}$ and angle XYZ = $90°$
14 a circle radius $3\,\text{cm}$ drawn with centre A
   b line equidistant between parallel lines
15 $15\,\text{cm}$, $22.5\,\text{cm}$ 16 $6\,\text{cm}$
17 $6.1\,\text{cm}$ to 1 d.p.   18 $7\sqrt{3}\,\text{cm}$
19 $90°$ anti-clockwise rotation about $(3, -1)$
20 a accurate drawing   b accurate drawing
21 $40\,\text{cm}^3$, $76\,\text{cm}^2$ 22 $254\,\text{mm}^3$, $226\,\text{cm}^2$
23 $56\,\text{cm}^3$
24 Accurate drawing of front, side and plan
25 $163\,\text{cm}^3$
26 a $\begin{pmatrix} 5 \\ 1 \end{pmatrix}$ b Accurate drawing

Bearings and scale drawings (page 59)

1 a Accurate drawing   b $230°$
2 a $2\,\text{km}$ b $26.8\,\text{cm}$ 3 $260°$

Compound units (page 60)

1 $918\,\text{km/hr}$
2 400 secs or 6 mins 40 sec   3 64 litres

Working with compound units (page 61)

1 3.72 person/km^2 increase

2 a $7.78\,\text{g/cm}^3$ b $11\,667\,\text{kg}$ or $11\,700$ to 3 s.f.
3 That it's travelling at 64.6 or 65 miles/hr

Types of quadrilateral (page 62)

1 $x = 45°$, $y = 135°$
2 ABCD is a rhombus or a parallelogram

Angles and parallel lines (page 63)

1 $x = 47°$ (x and 47 are alternate angles are equal), $y = 97°$ (y and 83 are supplementary angles, add up to 180)
2 $x = 52°$

Angles in a polygon (page 64)

1 $117°$ 2 by inspection

Congruent triangles and proof (page 65)

1 AC is common to AYC and AXC. AX = CY, given. AY = CX, perpendicular bisector of an equilateral triangle. So AYC and AXC are congruent (SSS).
2 by inspection

Proof using similar and congruent triangles (page 66)

1 AXD = BXD, vertically opposite angles. ADX = XBC, alternate angles. DAX = XCB, alternate angles. Both triangles have three equal angles so they are similar.
2 by inspection

Circumference and area of circles (page 67)

1 79.6 rotations   2 a $7.00\,\text{m}$ b $61.2\,\text{m}^2$

Pythagoras' theorem (page 68)

1 $7.6\,\text{cm}$ 2 $3855\,\text{m}$

Arcs and sectors (page 69)

1 $31\,\text{cm}$ 2 $2.57\,\text{cm}^2$

Mixed exam-style questions (page 70)

1 a $9\,\text{km}$ b by inspection   2 8 sides
3 AB = AC, BD = EC (given)

Angle ABC = angle ACB (isosceles triangle), SAS so ABD is congruent with ACE: therefore AD = AE so triangle ADE is isosceles

4 **a** 6820 revs 3 s.f. **b** 11.25 km/hr

5 Angle QPX = angle XTS (alternate angles), angle TSX = angle XQP (alternate angles), angle PXQ = angle SXT (vertically opp). PQX is similar to SXT (AAA) Corresponding sides equal, therefore triangles are congruent or Angle PQX=Angle TSX alternate angles are equal. Angle PXQ=Angle TXS vertically opposite angles are equal. QX=XS given. Triangles PQX and STX are congruent ASA

6 **a** scale drawing **b** 22.2 m² 3 s.f.
7 **a** 2.12 cm 3 s.f. **b** 1.28 cm²
8 **a** 10.5 cm 3 s.f. **b** 3.33 cm s.f.
9 PS=QR (given), PX = QX (isosceles triangles), SX=RX (isosceles triangles) PXS and QXR are similar SSS.
10 9.49 cm

Constructions with a pair of compasses (page 72)

1 **a** Accurately constructed right angled triangle
  b Accurately constructed angle bisector at A
  c BX = 3.5 cm
2 Accurate drawing of triangle XYZ such that XY = 9 cm, YZ = 6.5 cm and XZ = 7 cm.
3 **a** Perpendicular bisector of line PQ, (PX = XQ = 4.5 cm)
  b SX drawn = 5.7 cm **c** SPQ = 52°

Loci (page 73)

1 Accurate drawing
2 Intersection of perpendicular bisectors of 3 sides of XYZ

Enlargement (page 74)

1 Enlargement, sf 2, centre of enlargement (1, 5)
2 Accurate drawing

Similarity (page 76)

1 4 cm **2** 13.5 cm

Trigonometry (page 77)

1 **a** 68.2° **b** 3.2 m **2** 11.3 cm

Trigonometry for special angles (page 78)

1 **a** $6\sqrt{2}$ cm **b** $4\sqrt{6}$ cm **2** $32\sqrt{3}$ cm **3** 10 cm

Finding centres of rotation (page 79)

1 **a** (−2,0)

b 90° anti-clockwise rotation about (−2, 0)
2 90° clockwise rotation about (−1, −2)

Understanding nets and 2D representation of 3D shapes (page 81)

1 Accurate drawing **2** Accurate drawing

Volume and surface area of cuboids and prisms (page 82)

1 **a** 98.2 m³ **b** 9817 litres
2 **a** 6 cm² **b** 27 cm³ **c** 66 cm²
3 24 cm × 2 cm × 2 cm. 4 cm × 4 cm × 6 cm.
  4 cm × 12 cm × 2 cm. 2 cm × 8 cm × 6 cm

Enlargement in two and three dimensions (page 84)

1 **a** 810 cm² **b** 1 : 27 **2** 54 cm³ **3** 4.9 cm

Constructing plans and elevations (page 85)

1 Accurate drawing
2 **a** Accurate drawing **b** Accurate drawing

Surface area and 3D shapes (page 86)

1 6 cm
2 **a** 14 900 cm³ to 3 s.f. **b** 3900 cm² to 3 s.f.

Vectors (page 87)

1 **a** **i** $\begin{pmatrix} 7 \\ 0 \end{pmatrix}$ **ii** $\begin{pmatrix} 4 \\ -4 \end{pmatrix}$ **iii** $\begin{pmatrix} 6 \\ 4 \end{pmatrix}$ **iv** $\begin{pmatrix} 17 \\ 2 \end{pmatrix}$

  b **i** Accurate drawing of vector $\begin{pmatrix} -2 \\ 8 \end{pmatrix}$

   ii Accurate drawing of vector $\begin{pmatrix} 6 \\ 4 \end{pmatrix}$

2 **a** **i** $\begin{pmatrix} 6 \\ -1 \end{pmatrix}$ **ii** $\begin{pmatrix} -3 \\ -3 \end{pmatrix}$ **b** $\overrightarrow{PQ} + \overrightarrow{QR}$

3 by inspection

Mixed exam-style questions (page 89)

1 5.9 km
2 **a** by inspection **b** 51° **3** 16.7 g
4 approximate ratio moon to earth 1:13.45
5 **a** 35.1 cm² **b** 526 cm³
  c 3.90 cm² **d** 139 cm² (all 3 s.f.)
6 Perpendicular bisector of line joining two rocks
7 3.22 m
8 **a** accurate scale drawing of net
  b 50 cm² − 70 cm²
9 2.67 min **10** Accurate drawing
11 **a** $\overrightarrow{FE}$ is parallel to $\overrightarrow{AB}$ **b** $p + q$
  c $p + q + r$ **d** $-r - q$
12 rotation 180° about (0, 1)

Statistics and Probability

Pre-revision check (page 91)

1 **a** 2 **b** 2.45 **2** **a** $15 < x \leqslant 20$ **b** £14.75
3 **a** by inspection **b** 72.7% **c** increasing
4 120°

5 accurate frequency table
6 **a** Scatter plot
  b Positive correlation, since the older the tree the greater the trunk radius
  c **i** 55 − 65 cm

ii Not reliable – extrapolation or Could be reliable since it is not that far away from the original data values

7 a $\frac{3}{7}$ b $\frac{5}{7}$ **8** a $\frac{3}{12}$ b $\frac{4}{12}$

9 a $\frac{3}{20}$

b Either "yes, because the frequencies should be roughly equal" or "no, not enough spins to conclude whether this is true"

10 $\frac{14}{30}$ **11** a Accurate Venn diagram b $\frac{3}{50}$

Using frequency tables (page 93)

1 a 1 b 2 c 2.2 d 4
2 a 1 b 1 c 1.2 d 3

Using grouped frequency tables (page 95)

1 61.29 seconds (2 d.p.)
2 a $1 < w \leqslant 1.5$ b $1.5 < w \leqslant 2$
 c 1.73 kg (2 d.p.)

Vertical line charts (page 96)

1 a Accurate vertical line chart
 b It rained c £305.49
2 a Accurate vertical line chart
 b Yes, as significantly more 6s than other numbers OR Can't tell as more throws needed

Pie charts (page 97)

1 by inspection **2** 1260 grams

Displaying grouped data (page 98)

a Time taken can take any value in a given interval
b Accurate frequency table
c Accurate frequency diagram
d The median is the $\frac{25+1}{2} = 13$th value in the ordered data, which lies in the group $20 < t \leqslant 25$. The modal group is the group $20 < t \leqslant 25$, which contains the median. So Frantz is right.

Scatter diagrams and using lines of best fit (page 100)

a Accurate diagram b Negative correlation
c i 10.5 OC. Interpolation, so reliable (although small amount of data may make this unreliable)
 ii 700 metres. Extrapolation, so unreliable

Mixed exam-style questions (page 102)

1 a 5, 14, 10, 7, 4 b i 1 ii 2 iii 1.775
 c e.g. mean, as it includes all the data
2 a 48 b i $3 < w \leqslant 3.5$ ii $3 < w \leqslant 3.5$
 c i 3.29 kg ii 2
 d the mid-interval values are used to represent the data values in each class interval
3 a i Accurate vertical line chart ii Pie chart
 b Line chart, because it shows frequencies OR Pie chart, because it shows proportions
4 Pie chart: angles Wins 216°, Loses 90°, Draws 54°.
5 $\frac{3}{10}$ **6** 0.15 **7** a by inspection b $\frac{7}{30}$

Single event probability (page 104)

1 a $\frac{3}{10}$ b $\frac{7}{10}$ c 0
2 35% or 0.35 or $\frac{7}{20}$ **3** $\frac{4}{7}$ **4** 28

Combined events (page 105)

1 $\frac{17}{24}$ **2** $\frac{2}{19}$

Estimating probability (page 106)

1 a $\frac{14}{20}$ b 90 **2** $\frac{29}{60}$

The multiplication rule (page 107)

1 a by inspection b 0.005 c 0.045 **2** $\frac{11}{42}$

The addition rule (page 109)

1 a $\frac{6}{23}$ b $\frac{16}{23}$ c 0
2 a Accurate Venn diagram
 b $\frac{22}{67}$ c $\frac{49}{67}$ **3** a 0.4 b 0.9

Mixed exam-style questions (page 111)

1 a i 32 mph ii 27 b Accurate diagram
 c 40 mph. Most speeds are below 40 mph.
2 a Accurate scatter chart
 b (70, 70). Does not fit the pattern of the other data.
 c Positive correlation
 d i 82 – 84 minutes
  ii Reliable for data as interpolation, but may not be reliable overall as small sample of students.
3 3064 **4** a $\frac{1}{30}$ b $\frac{11}{30}$
5 $\frac{64}{105}$ **6** 0.032
7 a by inspection b 3 c i $\frac{3}{24}$ ii $\frac{15}{24}$